ICT PROJECTS FOR
G C S E

R.S.U. HEATHCOTE

Published by

PAYNE-GALLWAY
P U B L I S H E R S L T D

www.payne-gallway.co.uk

Acknowledgements

Cover picture © Heat of the Day reproduced with the kind permission of Clare Blois

Cover photography Mike Kwasniak, 160 Sidegate Lane, Ipswich

Photograph of School Sports Day reproduced with kind permission from the Headteacher, Ipswich Preparatory School.

Payne-Gallway is a division of Harcourt Education Ltd.

Linacre House, Jordan Hill, Oxford, OX2 8DP

Copyright © R.S.U. Heathcote 2002

First edition 2002. Reprinted 2003, 2005.

08 07 06 05
10 9 8 7 6 5 4 3

ISBN 1 903112 69 9

British Library Cataloguing in Publication data is available from the British Library on request.

Design and artwork by: Direction123.com

Printed in Malta by Gutenberg Press

Preface

Coursework requirements

Every GCSE ICT course involves practical project work. Students will have to complete between one and five projects using different software packages. This book is designed to help students choose suitable projects and complete the required stages for a top grade.

Do students need a projects book?

Students often have difficulty in every aspect of coursework from selecting a suitable project and analysing suitable requirements right through to documenting their final solution. They have difficulty understanding what the syllabus means, understanding how much has to be done in order to gain the marks in a particular section and how to plan their time so that the project is completed within a specified number of weeks. The most helpful resource that a teacher can give to a student is an A* grade sample project along the lines of what is required. All of us can make better and faster progress if we have a model to follow when attempting some new task, whatever that task may be.

The approach taken

Four different software packages are used in different projects. Ideas for projects in each of these packages are suggested and a full sample project is then shown providing a model of what is required. A checklist of points that should be covered is included to help students assess their own progress through the project. These checklists can be downloaded from the Payne-Gallway website and given out to the students.

What knowledge is assumed?

Some knowledge of the software packages is assumed, but each project is accompanied by a separate section called *Tips for implementation* which explains how to implement the project. Version 2002 of the Microsoft software has been used.

Which exam board specifications are covered?

The mark scheme followed is from the Edexcel full course specification. The book contains four projects of varying lengths and degrees of difficulty, and all the projects use sufficient advanced features to merit an A* in the Edexcel specification. Two of the projects (Access and Excel) are sufficiently complex and detailed to be submitted as a single project (e.g. for the AQA specification). Where four or five projects are being submitted, considerably less detail would be acceptable.

The book will also be a useful guide for students following the GCSE in Applied ICT (Double Award) for any of the Examining Boards.

Extra resources

You will find the extra resources to accompany this book which are mentioned in the text, at www.payne-gallway.co.uk/gcseproj.

Table of Contents

Introduction to Project Work

Coursework requirements

Every exam board has different coursework requirements, and you need to know which syllabus or specification you are using. For Edexcel, for example, you will have to write four different projects. This book contains four sample projects in PowerPoint, Access, Excel and Publisher, but you may choose to use different software.

Using the checklists

At the beginning of each section you will find suggestions for the type of projects you can choose, followed by a checklist of up to 40 items you should include to get an A* in the Edexcel specification. If you are following a different specification you may need to amend this checklist.

Download the checklist from www.payne-gallway.co.uk/gcseproj and study it carefully. Try to plan your time so that you can tick at least two or three items off each week. You will find this very helpful in getting your project completed.

Choosing your user

If possible, try and find a **real user** who has a problem you could solve for your project. It is best to find someone such as a parent, teacher or neighbour who will be easy to talk to and easy to find when needed.

If it is not possible to find a real user then you are allowed to make one up by using a friend in class, for example, to play the role of the real user. You are not allowed to pretend to be the user yourself!

Each project will have five stages – Identify, Analyse, Design, Implement and Evaluate. It is a good idea to start off your project by copying out the headings and subheadings from a relevant sample project before you start on yours. This will give you some idea of what needs to be done for the project and provide a structure for you to follow.

Here are the basic requirements for each section:

Identify   Find a user with an idea for a project and explain the problem

Analyse   Analyse what needs to be done to satisfy the user requirements

Design   Develop a solution for the problem

Implement   Implement and test the solution

Evaluate   Summarise how well the final solution meets the needs of the user

There are two different levels at which you can approach a task: standard and extension.

The extension task will involve using some of the more advanced features of the relevant software package in your solution. Only the extension level tasks can gain the top marks.

An Edexcel mark scheme and specification for the coursework is included at the back of this book.

Introduction to Project Work

The documentation

The report that you submit at the end of the project will be all that the examiner sees. It should therefore contain all the evidence of the work you have carried out. No matter how good your analysis, how appropriate your design, how clever the implementation and how thorough the testing; if the evidence isn't there to prove it, you will not get the marks.

It will take longer than you think to complete the documentation.

It is much easier to complete the written project if you keep the documentation up-to-date as you work through the 5 stages of project development. There will be countless things to say and points to make about each stage of the project that you will forget unless they are written down. Make sure you write down changes that you make or things that go wrong that you later correct.

Should the documentation be word-processed?

There is sometimes no strict guidance on whether you should type up your project or not, but a smartly presented project which is pleasant to read is much nicer for an examiner to mark than a badly thrown together collection of paper in illegible handwriting!

You will be given up to 8 extra marks for the quality of written communication in your projects. This focuses on presentation, clarity, spelling, punctuation and grammar – all of which are usually improved upon if the documentation has been typed. Remember to proofread your work carefully before handing it in.
Some errors, such as a misspelling in their, there or they're, will not be detected by the computer.

Screenshots

Some exam boards prefer you to include hand-drawn designs rather than screenshots as proof of your design. In your Implementation section include printed reports where possible, for example in an Access project, otherwise show screenshots. Annotate all your printed output and screenshots by hand to explain what they show.

If you need to take a screenshot, **Alt+Print Screen** will capture the active window and put the image on the clipboard. (**Print Screen** will capture the entire screen.) This can then be pasted into your Word document using **Edit**, **Paste** on the main menu.

Putting it all together

Your final project should be neatly bound in such a way that it can be easily read without the examiner having to unbind it. A ring binder will be too big for any of these projects and cannot be conveniently posted to the moderator. A single plastic cover with suitable binding is ideal.

Do not put each page (or several pages together) in a plastic sleeve; it makes the project report heavy, expensive to post, and inconvenient for marking.

PowerPoint

3

Choosing a Project

Introduction

A real user for a PowerPoint project is quite easy to find. Any shop, organisation, or company could make use of either a kiosk-style presentation which simply runs itself, or one where people can click buttons to find out different pieces of information. You could even use one of your teachers as your real user if they have to deliver a series of lessons and don't already use PowerPoint for this purpose.

Examples of some good ideas for a project are listed below:

- An information booth for tourist information
- A presentation to help advertise the school at a prospective parents' evening
- A presentation to advertise a product or service
- An interactive storyboard where the user can choose the outcome of the story

You should try to use buttons, animations, imported charts or graphs, or graphics manipulated in another package in order to gain top grades. PowerPoint is a relatively simple package and to demonstrate extension level skills you need to use most of the features it has. Some examples of standard and extension problem types are shown below:

Standard	Extension
Entering and editing text in text boxes	Importing data from another application
Changing font type and size	Image manipulation
Inserting clip art	Custom animations
Using different slide layouts	Slide transitions
Using drawing objects	Using the Slide Master
Changing text and background colours	Using action buttons

Poor Projects

Poor projects are generally those that are not ideally suited to PowerPoint or those which do not suit a presentation style of output.

You need to choose a topic that can be easily summarised in bullet points on a sequence of slides. Large blocks of text are not suitable for display on a screen.

Be careful in your choice of a suitable subject or topic on which to base your presentation. It is important to demonstrate all of PowerPoint's features, and to match the style of presentation to the topic. For example, if your presentation deals with a sensitive issue like famine in the Third World, it may be inappropriate to start jollying it up with flashy effects and sounds.

Using the checklist

On the next page you will find a checklist to help you ensure that you have included everything you need for a top grade. Keep it handy and refer to it throughout, ticking off items as you write them up in your project documentation.

Checklist for PowerPoint Project

Number	Section	Documentation	Done
1	Title page	Student name, title of project and type of software	
2	Identify (5 marks)	Section title	
3		Background detail	
4		User identified	
5		Statement of the problem	
6		Manual solution considered	
7		Two alternative software solutions considered	
8		Proposed solution justified	
9		At least 3 quantitative objectives identified	
10	Analyse (9 marks)	Section title	
11		Appropriate hardware identified	
12		Appropriate software identified	
13		Types and source of data explained (e.g. text information from user, maps, scanned photographs)	
14		Data manipulation explained (e.g. image manipulation in a Paint package or spreadsheet/chart imported)	
15		User input and navigation (e.g. menu, buttons) explained	
16		Alternative methods of output considered (e.g. screen, printer, speakers)	
17		Choice of output method justified	
18		Backup strategy identified	
19		Security strategy (e.g. password) explained	
20	Design (9 marks)	Section title	
21		Initial designs showing colour schemes, layout of slides and navigation between slides	
22		Menu structure diagram	
23		User feedback on initial designs (comments, letter or questionnaire results)	
24		Final design for slides justified	
25		Subtasks identified	
26		Each slide sketched out, showing content and buttons	
27		Security (e.g. password system) explained	
28		Test plan containing at least 10 tests and expected results	
29	Implement (12 marks)	Section Title	
30		Brief description of how the design was implemented, explaining any changes that had to be made to the design	
31		Hard copy of each slide, annotated to explain effects or animations	
32		Evidence that each test in the test plan was carried out, comparing actual results with expected results	
33		When errors occurred, explain how they were corrected	
34	Evaluate (5 marks)	Section Title	
35		Each original objective fully evaluated. Comment on how well the objectives are fulfilled	
36		Comment on any major problems that caused a change in design	
37		A critical comment on anything that you think could be improved	
38		User feedback in the form of a letter or questionnaire User comment should be critical and relevant	
39		Evidence that you understand the user's comments by making suggestions for future improvements	

GCSE ICT Project

PowerPoint

Tourist Information Display
Birchwood Campsite

A.Student

Part One - Identify

Part One - Identify

Statement of the problem

Mr and Mrs Hemmings are the owners of Birchwood Campsite. The campsite has space for 100 pitches, and washing facilities. There is also an office and shop.

They want an information system so that tourists who come to stay can find out about the site and surrounding area at any time of day without having to find a site representative.

Currently, the site shop is only open from 8am until 8pm. The shop has an information desk and reception as well as an area selling groceries. Whoever is running the store is also responsible for helping residents with their enquiries. This works well, but at peak times the shop can often get busy with shoppers and there is no-one available to help people making enquiries. Outside the shop opening times, there is nowhere for residents to go for information.

It is recognised that the *actual* users of the system will in fact be the guests staying at the campsite. Since they are not so easy to get in contact with, the owners of the site will be the users as far as this project is concerned.

Consideration of Alternative Solutions

- A booklet of the site and surrounding area could be produced in a word processor and copies issued to all guests at the site or left in a leaflet holder outside the shop after closing. Here, all the information would be available but guests would have to search through the guide for the information they really wanted and the leaflets might end up littering the site. The cost of producing leaflets would also be incurred each time the information was updated.

- A database could be used to create a series of forms that are connected using menus. This would be very good for such a guide as guests could home in on the information they were looking for by following the menus on each screen. Databases are very powerful programs, however, and it may seem like overkill to try and use such a system for a problem such as this.

- A presentation package would be very useful for producing an interactive information system about the campsite and its surrounding area. Several different features can be incorporated to add interest. You can animate different objects on the screen – for example text blocks can fly in from the top of the screen, or pictures can flash. This would be very good for an information display and even catch the attention of those who were not necessarily seeking information at the time. This type of system would have links to other pages, similar in operation to a website.

It is important to mention the user by name and give some explanation of what they do and the problems they face.

You may find it helpful to write down the user requirements before considering solutions.

At least one manual solution should be considered.

7

- Presentation software could also be used to create a self-running presentation by going to the next screen automatically at timed intervals. This would loop back to the start once it came to the end.

After consideration of each method I believe that the presentation package offers the best solution to the problem as it provides a great deal of flexibility in design solutions, is cheaper to buy than database software, and would be much easier for the owners of the campsite to maintain once I have finished this project.

Both the kiosk-style presentation, which loops over and over again, and a menu-driven system are better than a simple printed leaflet. Being able to animate screen objects would be a great addition to any information system and is also much easier to implement using presentation software rather than a database.

The user would prefer a menu-driven system to make the system interactive, so I will develop this type of system rather than a kiosk-style presentation.

User Requirements

I have spoken with the users, Mr and Mrs Hemmings, and they have specified several elements which they would like to see in the system and after discussion we have decided upon the following objectives:

1. The system must be interactive.
2. The system must use a system of buttons in order to navigate through the slides.
3. Each slide must contain a clear title.
4. Each slide must contain a button that will take the user back to the start.
5. The system must contain photographs of the campsite.
6. The campsite name and logo must appear on at least the title slide.
7. The system must include the following:
   General site information
   Information about the shop
   A schedule of weekly events
   A site map
   A local map
   Information about the local area
   A title screen or 'Home page'
8. Slides must include some animation effects.
9. The system must include transition effects when one slide changes to another.
10. The slides must be in colour.
11. It must not take more than 5 seconds for someone new to computers to learn how to use the system.

> Try to justify the best solution by comparing it with the strengths and weaknesses of the other suggestions.

> User requirements should be quantitative. This means that you should be able to measure exactly how well you achieved them in the Evaluate section at the end of the project.

Part Two - Analyse

Appropriate Software and Hardware

The package that I will be using will be Microsoft PowerPoint version 2002. This is the only software that will be needed, other than MS Windows in which it runs. PowerPoint is the leading presentation graphics program and comes with MS Office, which Mr Hemmings already owns.

A graphics program will also be used to manipulate the map image once it has been scanned in.

The hardware required will be a scanner with which to scan in some of the photographs that have been taken around the site, and a digital camera which I can borrow to take some more pictures of the surrounding area. These can be imported into PowerPoint directly from the camera using the *Insert, Picture, From Scanner or Camera* command on the menu.

A scanner will also be required to scan in the campsite map and a simple map of the area so guests have a good idea of how far everything is from the site.

A good monitor will be required since this information system will probably be running 24 hours a day. With this in mind it will also be necessary to use a screen-saver built in to MS Windows in order to preserve the screen. A custom screen-saver could be added at a later date.

Lastly, a good mouse will be required for guests to navigate the system by clicking on the buttons.

Data Required

The owners of the campsite will be able to tell me all of the required information about the site. More details about areas outside the site could be gathered from the Tourist Board in the nearest town. A map of the local towns will also need to be scanned in to show where the different areas are, and the location of the campsite marked on it.

A chart showing the information that I will need and where it will come from is shown below:

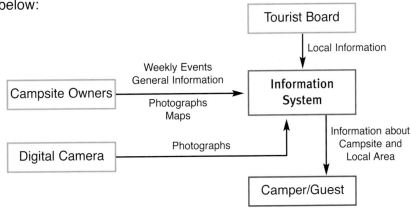

> If you will be needing any graphics or utility programs, then you will need to mention these here and why you will need them.

> There is no need to mention all the hardware that comes with a basic PC package but you must include details of any other hardware you will use.

> It is important to explain where all the information you will need to complete the system will come from. A diagram is sometimes a good way to do this.

Part Two - Analyse

PowerPoint 1

> Data manipulation means that you collected some data or a graphic and changed it before you put it into your presentation.

Data Manipulation

The scanned map of the campsite area can be imported into a Paint package and a red cross and label "You are here" added. Unnecessary detail from the map can be deleted and icons such as '**P**' for car parking added.

Information gathered about the campsite will be typed in and formatted with appropriate fonts and colours.

Data Flow

Updating site information

Mr Hemmings updates the site information whenever it changes. The new information is then stored in the application file.

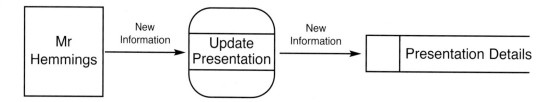

Dealing with customer enquiries

There will be a menu system with option buttons. A customer requests information from the system by clicking on a button. The system finds and displays the information for the customer.

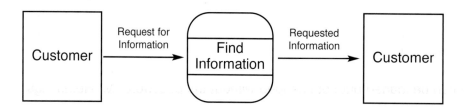

Format of information and graphics

There will be around 7-8 slides in order to display all the information. Each slide will contain at least one picture or animation to keep the interest of the camper.

The user requirements state that there should be a clear title on every slide. This should be in a larger font and in a different colour from the rest of the text.

All buttons used on the slides should be kept in the same place on every slide. This will ensure that the viewer will always know where to expect the '**Back to Start**' button to be on the page, making it easier to use.

The interface should not use too many colours. A uniform look should be chosen and adhered to. Likewise, the selection of animations and transitions must be restricted so that everything does not look all jumbled together. These constraints will all add to the system looking more professional in the end.

10

Output

The system will be permanently displayed on a computer monitor. The monitor should be fairly large and of high resolution. This means that photographs will be displayed properly and that detail can be seen.

Alternative forms of output could include an interactive screen in which customers can see the information on a big screen and still have the facility to make an input.

Ideally, a touch screen would be good. This would be expensive but would do away with the need for a mouse. This is something the Hemmings can look into in the future.

There will be no speakers attached to the computer because sounds can become very annoying when they are played over and over again in a public area.

A printer is not required since all information will be displayed on-screen. Customers can write down any information they are unable to remember. A printer would add extra cost to the implementation of the system.

Backup / security strategy

The computer file containing the presentation must be backed up onto floppy disk each time the system is updated. This copy should be kept at a different location from the computer hard disk that the presentation is stored on, in case there is a fire or flood at the premises. A backup copy also needs to be made when the system is first installed on Mr Hemmings's computer hard drive.

Since there can be many different people on the campsite at a time, some of the main computer hardware needs to be protected from vandalism or tampering. The CPU and keyboard should be locked away from the residents because they will not need access to these pieces of equipment. Only the mouse will be needed to operate the system.

A password could be added to the system to make it read-only. This way the presentation can be loaded but not changed without the password. Mr Hemmings should use a password that is personal to him and not too easy for someone else to guess.

You need to consider what form the output from your system will take. Will it be printed or on-screen? Will it use sound? Consider every possibility and state which output method your system will use.

Consider what method of backup you will use and state how often these backups should be made and why.

If you are using a password for security, you should mention some of the things that the user should be aware of in keeping the password a secret.

Part Three - Design

Part Three - Design

Initial Designs

The general idea of this system is for it to behave in a similar way to an Internet website. This means that viewers will be able to navigate through the information themselves and control what they are looking at.

The users are not expected to have any major experience of using computers before, nor are they expected to read a manual on how to use the system before finding something of interest on it. This means that the site needs to have a friendly interface which is quick and easy to use. It should not take anyone more than 5 seconds to figure out how to use the system.

The presentation should look attractive and interesting. The three major factors in achieving this are the font styles, the colour scheme and the design of the pages themselves.

Here are the different fonts that will be considered for use:

A. **BIRCHWOOD CAMPSITE**

B. **Birchwood Campsite**

C. **BIRCHWOOD CAMPSITE**

Using the various fonts and colour schemes, three design templates were sketched out. This gives the end users an idea of the look and feel of the system. They can then choose which one they like, or which parts they like of each and then a final design can be drawn up taking their preferences into account.

> It is good to produce more than one initial design to give the user some choice before deciding upon their favourite solution.

It is a good idea to include some hand-drawn preliminary sketches.

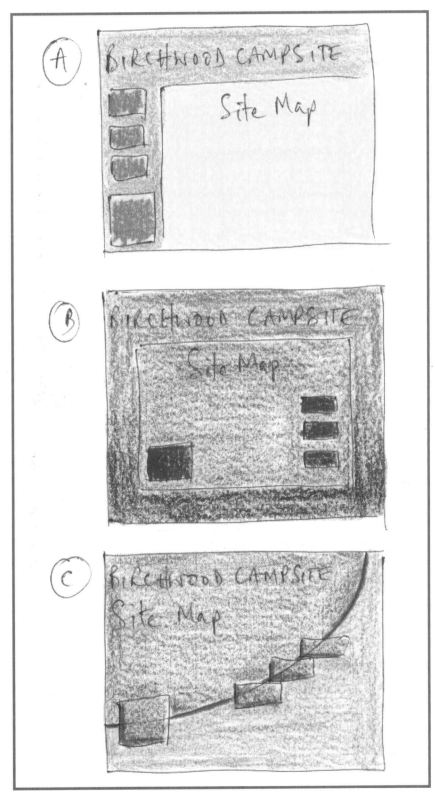

Initial designs for presentation

User Feedback on Initial Designs

The visitors staying at the campsite were given a short questionnaire asking them which design, font style and colour scheme they preferred. Ten people were interviewed.

The questions asked were as follows:

1. Which overall design do you like the best (A-C)?
2. Which font do you prefer (A-C)?
3. Which colour scheme do you prefer (A-C)?

This is one way of collecting feedback. You could also choose to get a letter from the user or conduct a short interview.

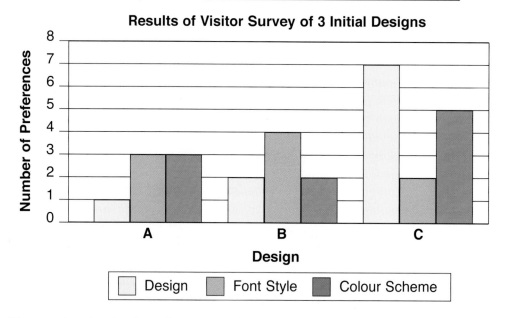

The results clearly show that generally design C was most popular. The colour scheme used in this design was also thought to be one of the best. Several people said that they preferred the green or brown colour scheme since it was a woodland area and they thought it went well. Font style B was thought to be the nicest.

In view of these results, I will adapt the third design so that it uses font style B.

The owners of the site also said that they thought the third design was the best. They were very happy with the choice of font and colours made by the guests. One comment they made about the third design was that the title was slightly too big and that the curve could be a little lower down the page since it takes up too much of the page. This would leave more room for the page content.

Part Three - Design

Menu Structure

The structure of the system also needs to be considered. This must begin with a title page or 'Home page' which the user can return to at any time or which a new user can go back to so they can begin using the system from the start.

The initial user requirements stated that, in addition to a title screen, 6 main topics of information need to be included.

It is important to include a menu tree to show how each slide links to the others.

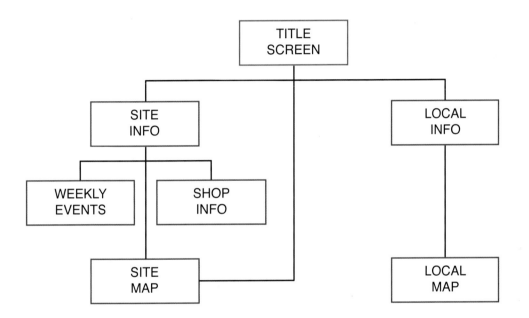

This design means that site information, local information and a site map can all be accessed directly from the title screen.

Final Design

Here are the drawings for the final design of the system.

The first three slides of this system are shown here. In your project, you will need to include a detailed drawing of every slide in your presentation.

If you choose to draw final designs in black and white, then you will also need to show which colours will be used where on the designs.

Use a whole page for each of your final designs.

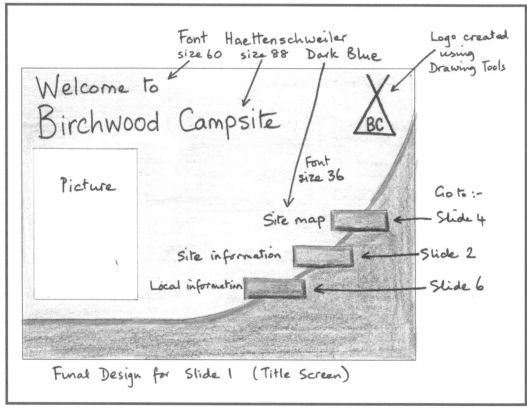

Final design: Slide 1

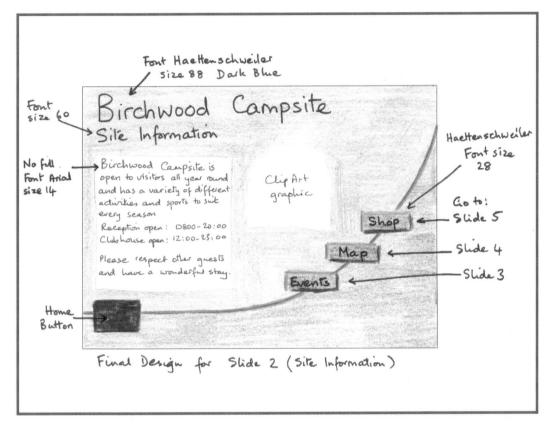

Final design: Slide 2

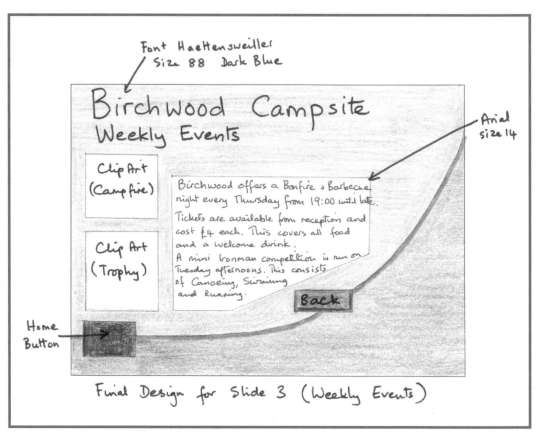

Final design: Slide 3

Part Three - Design

Animation and Transition Effects

The Option buttons on slides 2 to 7 will fly in from the right hand side one at a time until they come to a stop in their correct position. The Home buttons will have no animation.

When a button is clicked, the current slide will fade out into black and the new slide will fade in. This transition is called **Fade through Black** and will be applied to all slides in the system.

Breakdown of final solution into sub-tasks

The implementation of the final design can be broken down into sub-tasks.

Task 1: Create the title slide

The background graphics on the title slide will be created using tools on the Drawing toolbar. Text will be typed in the chosen font and a suitable photograph imported from the digital camera. The logo will be created using Drawing tools.

Task 2: Create the remaining slides

Copy slide 1 and type the text for Slide 2, replacing the existing text. Make the other slides in a similar way.

Task 3: Add area maps

Scan the area maps and manipulate them in Paint. Insert the maps in the appropriate slides.

Task 4: Add buttons

Add Home buttons to slides 2 to 7. Place other navigation buttons as shown in the design.

Task 5: Add animation and transitions to each slide

These effects are added to make the presentation more interesting.

Task 6: Test the system

Implement the test plan and correct any errors.

Test Plan

In order to make sure that the design contains all the information required, that there are no errors and it fulfils the requirements specified by the user, a test plan has been devised. This will be implemented once the designs have been implemented.

Be sure to mention anything that is not obvious from your final designs. They should be detailed enough for another person to use to implement your system on the computer.

Refer to the user requirements when writing a test plan and make sure you have done everything. Include tests to make sure everything works as planned, and that you have no spelling or grammar errors.

Test	Purpose of test	Test method	Expected result
1	Test system security.	Load system	Password should be requested. Only *Birchwood* accepted.
2	Test Site Map button, Site Map slide transition and button animation.	Click on Site Map button	Site map screen should fade in through black. Back button should fly in from the right.
3	Test Back button on Site Map slide and transition on Home page.	Click the Back button.	The Home page should be re-displayed with fade transition. .
4	Test the Site Information button, slide transition and button animation.	Click on the button.	Site Information slide displayed with fade transition. All buttons except Home button fly in from the right.
5	Test the Shop button.	Click on the Shop button.	The Shop slide should be displayed.
6	Test the Home button on the Shop slide.	Click Home.	The Home slide should fade in.
7	Test the Local Information button.	Click on the button.	Local Information slide should be displayed, with fade transition and animated buttons.
8	Test the rest of the buttons in a similar systematic way.	Click each button, noting the result.	All buttons work correctly with animated buttons and fade transition between slides.
9	Test spelling and grammar on each slide.	Run the spellchecker and then visually proofread each slide for grammar errors and correct content.	Spelling and grammar fine. All content required by the user was present.
10	Test whether a viewer can change the slide content.	Load the system as read-only and try to change the slide content.	Not possible to change the content without a password.
11	Test whether a viewer finds the system easy to use.	Ask someone to try out system.	The tester had no problems in using the system and said he 'instinctively knew how to use it'.

Part Four - Implement

Finished Design

The finished design was relatively straightforward to implement, but a major change needed to be made to the template. This was because the large curving background design took up far too much of the slide to allow enough space for the slide content. This was changed to a simple border across the bottom, which still looks good and is an effective design.

Slide 1:

Slide 1: The title slide

You must annotate, **by hand**, the printouts of your finished presentation. Show how the project developed, mention errors discovered during implementation, describe changes to the final design and suggest areas for improvement.

Slide 2:

Slide 2: The Site Information slide

The curved design used on the first slide had to change to accommodate more information.

Slide 3:

Slide 3: The Weekly Events slide

The site owner decided that he wanted more information added to the slide.

Slide 4:

The map was scanned and imported into Paint, and the "X You are here" was added. The picture was then imported into PowerPoint.

The "Back" button was meant to go back to the previous slide visited but instead, will take you to slide 3.

Slide 4: The Site Map slide

Slide 5:

Slide 5: The Shop Information slide

Slide 6:

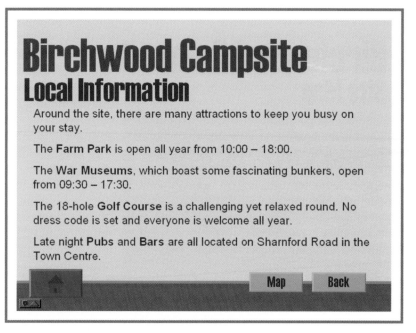

Slide 6: The Local Information slide

Slide 7:

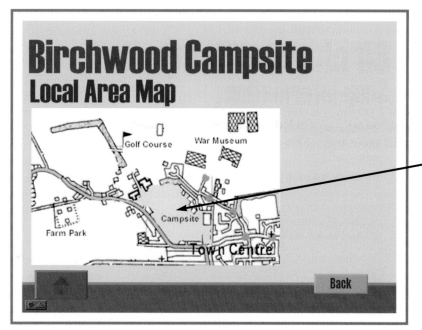

The map could be improved to show the route into town and include some information about the attractions such as prices and opening times.

Slide 7: The Local Area Map slide

Test Results

The test plan devised in the design section has been implemented.

Test	Purpose of test	Expected result	Actual result
1	Test system security.	Password should be requested. Only *Birchwood* accepted.	Password window appeared. Birchwood accepted as shown below.

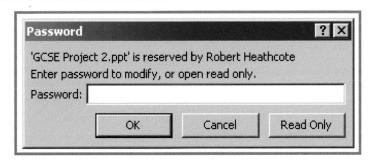

Test 1

You should include any evidence that the tests were carried out, showing the outcome.

Test	Purpose of test	Expected result	Actual result
2	Test Site Map button, Site Map slide transition and button animation.	Site map screen should fade in through black. Back button should fly in from the right.	Site map was displayed. The buttons did fly in, and one at a time, but the timing seemed to be too much in between each button. Once the timings had been reduced it worked very well.
3	Test Back button on Site Map slide and transition on Home page.	The Home page should be re-displayed with fade transition.	The Back button takes the user to the Site Information, which is the previous screen in numeric sequence but not necessarily the previous screen visited.
4	Test the Site Information button, slide transition and button animation.	Site Information slide displayed with fade transition. All buttons except Home button fly in from the right.	As expected. However the second time this test was performed the button animation did not work. It only happens the first time the buttons are displayed.

A detailed comparison of the expected and actual results is important in testing.

Test	Purpose of test	Expected result	Actual result
5	Test the Shop button.	The Shop slide should be displayed.	As expected.
6	Test the Home button on the Shop slide.	The Home slide should fade in.	As expected.
7	Test the Local Information button.	Local Information slide should be displayed, with fade transition and animated buttons.	As expected.
8	Test the rest of the buttons in a similar systematic way.	All buttons work correctly with animated buttons and fade transition between slides.	Back buttons do not always go to the expected slides.
9	Test spelling and grammar on each slide.	Spelling and grammar fine. All content required by the user was present.	Some spelling mistakes corrected.
10	Test whether the user can change the slide content.	Not possible to change the content without a password.	User can end the show but cannot make any changes - text and graphics cannot be selected.
11	Can the user easily use the system?	The system is very easy to use and takes no time to learn.	The tester had no problems in using the system and said he 'instinctively knew how to use it'.

Part Five - Evaluate

Part Five - Evaluate

Evaluation of Initial Objectives

1. The system is interactive, allowing the user to click on buttons to see the information they need. The buttons link each slide to the Home slide and up to three others according to the menu structure laid out in the Design section.

2. All information required in the system has been included and illustrated with several graphics. The photograph of the campsite was not very satisfactory. The photo needs to be taken again and substituted. The campsite's logo is displayed in the top right-hand corner of the title slide.

3. The animation of the buttons is very effective and works well. It turns out however that this only happens the first time a slide is viewed. This is a feature of PowerPoint and it cannot be changed.

4. The slides use an appealing colour scheme and have a uniform look that is quite professional and interesting.

5. Several people tried the system and found it easy to use. This is excellent because it means that more people on the campsite can access the information they need.

> Make sure that you refer back to the original user requirements in the Identify section when evaluating your solution.

User Feedback on Solution

Mr Hemmings was given the finished system to have a look at and he sent back the letter shown below:

Birchwood Campsite

Lower Lane, Pannington, Cumbria CA23 5LU
Tel: 01253 360976   Fax: 01253 360665
Proprietor: J.L. Hemmings

Dear Sir,

I am most impressed with your PowerPoint presentation for my campsite guests, which I think they will find very easy to use and informative. The only items I would change are:

— on the Events page, Canoeing does not need a capital 'C';

— on the Local Information page, the attractions would look better as bullet-points, or indented.

Apart from these, I am most satisfied and feel that this will add greatly to visitors' enjoyment.

yours sincerely

JL Hemmings

Further Ideas for Improvements

The system could be improved with the addition of another slide for weekly events as suggested by the user. This could either be updated each morning with the day's activities or a library of slides with different daily events could be designed and an appropriate one could be added to the system each morning to replace the one from the day before.

The corrections highlighted by Mr Hemmings in his letter also need to be made in order to improve the system further.

Ideally, a touch screen would be perfect for this sort of system. This would do away with the need for a mouse and a surface on which to use it. A touch screen system could be mounted in the wall of the shop instead of on a table, saving space.

A printer could also be added so that visitors could print out either of the maps shown in the system and take them away. It is difficult to memorise where things are from a map so this would be very useful to some people, especially if they are going off site into the local town.

Any ideas for improvement should be based on your own evaluation of the objectives, comments from the user and some more of your own suggestions.

Tips for Implementation

This chapter will show you how to build the PowerPoint project. By following the instructions, you will acquire the skills necessary to implement your own project.

The opening screen background

You may choose to use an existing template for your project, or you could start with a blank slide and design your own background. That is what you will do here.

- Load Microsoft PowerPoint and select **Blank Presentation**.

- From the choices offered for **Layouts**, select a completely blank slide.

- From the Formatting toolbar, select the **Zoom** tool and specify **50%**. This will give you more room around the page in which to place shapes that will overlap the edge of the slide.

- Click the **Oval** tool on the Drawing toolbar and draw a large oval shape.

- Colour the shape pale green and give it a thick green border.

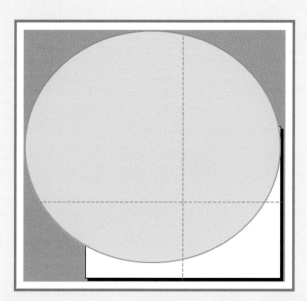

Figure 1.1: Creating an oval that overlaps the slide

- Use a combination of lines and rectangles to create a straight edge from the border of the oval to the edges of the slide.

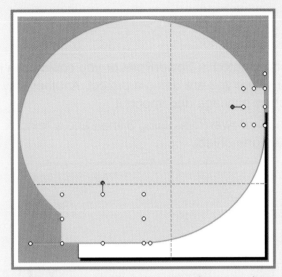

Figure 1.2: Adding lines and rectangles

You may need to use the **Send to Back** function. Right-click the object you want to send to back and select **Order**. This can help to get the background looking as good as possible.

Finally, the white area behind the shapes needs to be shaded.

 Right click the white area at the bottom of the slide and select **Background…**

 Click **More Colors…** and select a dark shade of green.

Adding content to the opening screen

Now you are ready to start adding content to the slide. This information system will need a title, a picture of the campsite, the company logo and buttons that link to other pages.

 Place a textbox in the top left corner of the slide (not the top left of the oval!) Remember that the viewable area is smaller than your oval. Type *Welcome to*.

 Change the font to **Haettenschweiler** and increase the size to **60**.

 Create another textbox below the first and type *Birchwood Campsite*. Make this **Haettenschweiler**, size **88**.

 Change the text colour of both lines to Dark Blue.

 Check the slide in **Slide Show** view. Make any adjustments necessary at this stage.

Creating a logo

The logo can either be created in PowerPoint or you could scan in a logo of an existing company for which you are doing a project. Another way would be to create one in a graphics package and import it.

This logo was created in PowerPoint using 3 lines and a textbox. These were then grouped to make them one object.

Figure 1.3: Inserting a picture

Later on, navigation buttons will be added to this screen.

 View this screen in Slide Show View.

Figure 1.4: The opening screen in Slide Show view

Inserting more slides

The rest of the slides in the information system are going to be given a slightly different look from the opening screen. To do this, a new blank slide is designed and then copied each time an additional slide is needed.

▶ Click on **Insert**, **New Slide**. Select the **Blank** layout.

▶ Make a large rectangle without a border in the same way as you created the rectangles on the first slide. This time allow the rectangle to fill the entire slide except for a small gap at the bottom. This bit you can shade in with the dark green background used before.

▶ Right-click the white area and select **Background...** to fill it in dark green.

▶ Click the **Apply to All** button. This means all future slides will have a green background.

▶ Select the first slide and select the **Birchwood Campsite** textbox. Right-click its border and select **Copy** from the shortcut menu.

▶ Return to slide 2 and right-click the slide. Choose **Paste**. Move the text into position at the top left of the slide.

Figure 1.5: Slide 2

▶ Now insert another text box with the text *Site Information* under the title.

▶ Underneath this, add some text about the site. For this exercise you can just type in anything.

Figure 1.6: Slide 2 - Site Information

▶ Add some Clip Art to the right of the slide by clicking **Insert**, **Picture**, **Clip Art** from the main menu. Alternatively use the **Insert Clip Art** button on the Drawing toolbar.

▶ You may find the Microsoft Clips Online website a useful source for more original pictures. It has a much bigger selection than most individual computers.

Adding a third slide

As mentioned earlier, the easiest way to get another slide with the same look is to copy an existing one and then delete or change the relevant objects to suit the design of the new slide.

▶ In Normal View, right-click the second slide in the left hand pane and click **Copy** on the shortcut menu. You can also perform this operation in Slide Sorter View.

▶ Right-click a blank area underneath the existing slides and select **Paste**. A copy of slide 2 should appear.

▶ Select the new slide.

▶ Select the text box by clicking on the border of the box and press **Delete** on the keyboard.

▶ Delete the picture as well.

▶ Insert a map image of the campsite. You may want to use the same picture as shown in Figure 1.7. This is available on the Payne-Gallway website. To insert the image use **Insert**, **Picture**, **From File...** on the main menu and search for the picture.

If you do not have this picture, use a suitable image instead for this step.

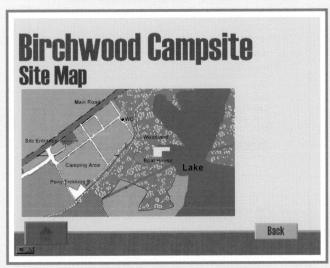

Figure 1.7: Slide 3 - Site Map

▶ Save the presentation so far.

▶ Add further slides in the same way as you created this slide. This section will only add the first three in order to demonstrate the techniques used.

Adding buttons

Buttons allow the user the flexibility to navigate through the slides in your presentation without having to view each slide in turn. They are similar to those used in websites or information booths.

▶ Select the first slide.

▶ Click **Slide Show**, **Action Buttons** and select the first, blank button.

▶ Click and drag a small rectangular-shaped button on the right hand side of the slide, over the bright green arc.

▶ The Action Settings window will appear. Click **Hyperlink to**: and select **Slide...** from the list of options.

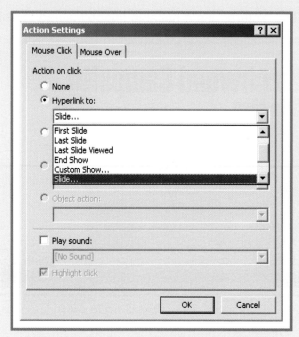

Figure 1.8: The Action Settings window

 Now select **Slide 3**, the site map, from the selection of slides available.

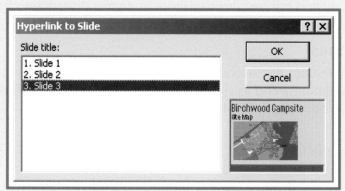

Figure 1.9: Linking an action button to slide 3

 Click **OK**.

 Click the **Slide Show** button in the bottom left corner of the screen and test your new button. If it works you should go straight to the site map slide, missing out the slide with site information.

 Press **Escape** on the keyboard to end the show.

Now you need to put a button on the site map slide (slide 3) to take you back to the first slide.

Tips for Implementation

Adding a Home button

A Home button will automatically take you back to the first slide in your presentation.

Make sure that the third slide is selected and click on **Slide Show**, **Action Buttons**.

Click the second button, **Action Button: Home**.

Click and drag a small rectangular-shaped button in the bottom left of the slide. You will see the Action Settings window automatically appear.

Check that **Hyperlink to: First Slide** is selected and click **OK**.

Run the slide show to test the new button.

Exit the show.

Formatting a button

Make sure that slide 1 is selected and double-click the button.

Select a new colour for the button. You can also add a line or border.

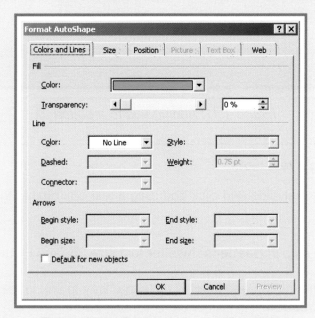

Figure 1.10: Formatting an action button

Change the colour of the **Home** button on slide 3.

Creating a Hot Spot

If you want to turn an area of a picture into a button (but not the whole picture) then you can make a button to fit over the area and format it as having **No Fill**. This will make it invisible so it looks as though you are actually clicking on the picture.

Creating an action object

If you would like an entire object such as a picture or text box to act like a button, then simply right-click the object and select **Action Settings** from the shortcut menu. The rest is easy.

Labelling a button

You can either choose to add text directly onto a button or you can put a label next to it, whichever you feel looks best. This exercise will show you both methods.

Method 1: Adding text to a button

▶ Select the third slide and right-click the **Home** button in the bottom left corner.

▶ Click **Add Text** and type *Home*.

▶ Highlight the text and format it as **Haettenschweiler**, size **32**. Make it dark blue.

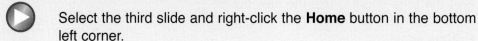
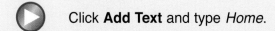

Figure 1.11: Adding text to a button

Method 2: Adding a text label

▶ Select the first slide and click and drag a text box next to the button on the right.

▶ Type *Site Map* in **Haettenschweiler** font size **36** (see Figure 1.12).

▶ Add another button and label in the same way to link to the second slide: **Site Information**.

Figure 1.12: Adding labels

 On Slide 2, add another **Home** button and text in the same way to link it to the Title slide.

Adding animation

You can animate almost anything in a PowerPoint slide. For this presentation you will animate the buttons so that they fly onto the screen from the right hand side.

 Select the first slide and right-click the **Site Map** button.

 Select **Custom Animation...**

Figure 1.13: Animating objects

▶ The Custom Animation window will appear. (See Figure 1.13.) Click the **Add Effect** button.

▶ Select **Entrance**, **Fly In**.

▶ Now select **After Previous** from the Start box.

▶ Select **From Right** in the Direction box.

▶ Click **Play** to test your animations.

▶ Close the Custom Animation window and run the show.

Adding slide transitions

Transitions are the way one slide changes into the next.

▶ Make sure you are in Normal View. Right-click the thumbnail image of slide 1 in the window on the left of the screen.

▶ Select **Slide Transition…**

▶ From the Apply to selected slides box, select **Fade Through Black**.

▶ Click **Apply to All Slides** so that you get a uniform effect throughout the presentation.

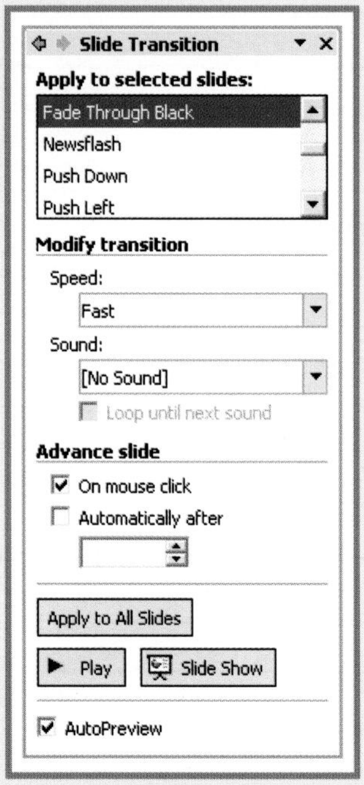

Figure 1.14: Adding slide transitions

Close the Slide Transition window and run your show from the beginning to see all your effects put together.

Adding a password

You can add passwords either to stop anyone from opening the file at all or to let them open the file but restrict any changes from being made to it.

Make sure that the presentation you have made is open.

 Click **Tools**, **Options** on the main menu.

 Select the **Security** tab.

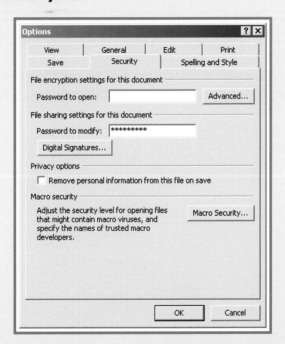

Figure 1.15: Adding a password for read-only access

 Enter a password in the **Password to modify** box. This will let anyone open it but they cannot change anything without knowing the password.

It is important to remember that passwords are CASE-SENSITIVE. Choose an **easy-to-remember** password for your system. This one is *'birchwood'*. Anything more complicated than that, and you may never be able to change your work again should you forget it.

 Once you have entered your password you will be asked to re-enter it for verification.

Figure 1.16: Password verification

All you need to do now is add more slides to complete the project. You can do this on your own – or begin designing a new presentation of your choice.

Access

Choosing a Project

Introduction

Identifying a real user for this sort of project isn't always easy. Most people needing a database are likely to want a more complicated one than you have time to make for this project. You are allowed to have a fictitious user, who could be role-played by a classmate, but a real one is better. Some examples of good database ideas are given below:

- A video shop database, where member, video and rental details are stored
- A doctor's or dentist's surgery holding information on patients, doctors and appointments
- A dating agency with details of single men, single women and dates
- An animal adoption centre with information on animals, adopters and adoptions

There are many, many others. Just ask your teacher.

All of the above ideas will involve related tables. This is one of the main things that will get you into the extension bracket. A report based on a query of more than one table will also do it. Some examples of standard and extension problem types are shown below. It is not necessary to do all of the things suggested in the extension column. They are only suggestions and one or two will be sufficient to pass the project as extension provided the documentation is there to support it.

Standard	Extension
Create the data files	Complex searches (eg. AND/OR)
Search the database	Reports from more than one file
Sort the database	Related tables
Generate reports	Macros

Some poor project ideas are:

Designing a database to replace an appointments system. It is very difficult in Access to build an appointments system where there will be more than one appointment in a day. It is fine to make a system for a hairdresser's or a doctor's surgery as long as you don't try to automatically find the available times in the day specified. You would simply have to type in the time and day and manually check for any clashes.

Designing a sales database. This will be a little too ambitious a project for most people since a proper ordering system would typically need more than 3 tables and some complicated queries to generate invoice reports. It is better to try and aim for something you know you can achieve rather than find yourself overwhelmed and unable to finish the task to a high standard.

The best advice is to talk to your teacher and agree the subject, table structures and relationships with them before doing anything *on the project.*

Use the checklist on the next page as you work through your project!

Checklist for Access Project

Number	Section	Documentation	Done
1	**Title page**	**Student name, title of project and type of software**	
2	**Identify (5 marks)**	**Section title**	
3		Background detail, identifying the user	
4		Statement of the problem	
5		Manual solution considered	
6		Two alternative software solutions considered	
7		Proposed solution justified	
8		At least 3 quantitative objectives identified	
9	**Analyse (9 marks)**	**Section title**	
10		Appropriate hardware identified	
11		Appropriate software identified	
12		Data collection and input (source data identified and explained, with details of input method, validation and key identifiers)	
13		Data flow diagrams showing data sources, processes and destinations	
14		Fields required, searches, sorts and reports that will be needed	
15		Alternative methods of output considered (e.g. screen, printer, speakers)	
16		Choice of output method justified	
17		Backup strategy identified	
18		Security strategy (e.g. password) explained	
19	**Design (9 marks)**	**Section title**	
20		Initial designs of input forms and reports sketched out	
21		Menu structure diagram	
22		User feedback on initial designs (comments, letter or questionnaire results)	
23		Final designs take user comments into account	
24		Table structures and relationships defined	
25		Form designs sketched in detail	
26		Queries explained in detail	
27		Reports sketched in detail	
28		Subtasks identified	
29		Test plan of up to 20 tests and expected results	
30	**Implement (12 marks)**	**Section Title**	
31		Brief description of how the design was implemented, explaining any changes that had to be made to the design	
32		Printouts of each report, with screenshots of forms and menus	
33		Evidence that each test in the test plan was carried out, comparing actual results with expected results	
34		When errors occurred, explain how they were corrected	
35	**Evaluate (5 marks)**	**Section Title**	
36		Each original objective fully evaluated. Comment on how well the objectives are fulfilled	
37		A critical comment on anything that you think could be improved	
38		User feedback in the form of a letter or questionnaire	
39		Evidence that you understand the user's comments by making suggestions for future improvements	

GCSE ICT Project

MS Access

Student Mark
Record System

A.Student

Part One - Identify

Statement of the problem

Mrs Knight is a Geography teacher at Kingswood School. She teaches all years from 7 up to 11 and keeps a very good record of all her pupils' marks in her register. Unfortunately, however accurate and well organised her records are, she cannot easily get good enough information out of them. For example, it would be very useful if all the student marks were given as a percentage as well as the actual mark they receive. Mrs Knight could then see exactly how well a student has done on a particular piece of work or see a trend in how they are progressing. Average grades are also time-consuming to calculate.

Another problem is that on a parents' evening she is unable to show a parent the list of their son's or daughter's marks without exposing some of the other students' marks from her record book.

After reading the statement of the problem, the reader should have a clear idea of who the user is, what the problems are and what is done at the moment.

Consideration of Alternative Solutions

One solution for Mrs Knight would be to add a few more columns to her mark book and work out all her pupils' average grades by hand. A list can then be made from her record book for each pupil to keep an individual's grades private.

An alternative solution would be to use a spreadsheet to log all the pupils' names, their marks and all the different assignments they are set. Calculations could then be made to find percentage marks and averages. This solution should not increase the amount of time already spent keeping marks in order but it would not be easy to produce reports on individuals without other students' grades being visible.

A third option is to use a database. This could perform the simple calculations required and also display a report on a particular individual.

The database solution is the best as it has better potential to solve the whole problem and should not increase the amount of time currently spent on record-keeping.

This section is much easier to read if alternative solutions are put in separate paragraphs.

User Requirements

Mrs Knight gave me a book of sample marks, recorded in a similar fashion to those that she keeps and also gave me her exact expectations of the new system.

1. The database must have a simple menu of options to choose from
2. Pupils' names must be listed in alphabetical order
3. All marks must be converted into a percentage
4. All students must be given an average percentage mark
5. It must take less than 5 seconds to enter each student's grade for a new assignment

Make sure you state which solution you are going to use and why. It is a good idea not to mention which database package you are going to use at this stage. This needs to be discussed in the Analyse section.

6. The system must be secure from access by pupils or unauthorised users
7. The system must be able to produce a printout of an individual's grades
8. The system must be able to produce a class list of grades for a particular assignment
9. The system must record the type of assignment, for example, homework, test and exam

Part Two - Analyse

Appropriate Software and Hardware

There are two different database software packages that are available to me. These are Microsoft Access and Microsoft Works database. Microsoft Works is a very simple version of its bigger brother, Access. Some of the requirements of this system are not possible to implement using Works so I will use Access. Access is a relational database, which will make it possible to link the tables needed for this database.

Hardware requirements are a basic PC package, including the PC itself, mouse and keyboard. Data will have to be input manually using a keyboard and mouse. A printer will also be needed to print reports.

Data collection and input

Mrs Knight will need to enter the following data:

- A list of the students in each class. This will be obtained at the start of the school year from a list produced by the school database. Each pupil will be assigned a unique ID (StudentID) and his or her class, surname and first name will be keyed in.

- Details of each assignment. These will be keyed in when each assignment is decided on, at various times during the school year. The data will be Assignment title, description, date to be handed in, assignment type (e.g. exam, homework) and maximum mark.

- The marks obtained by each student for a particular assignment. These will be keyed in after the assignment has been marked. The StudentID and the mark achieved will be entered and the system will validate the data to make sure that the mark is not greater than the maximum mark for this assignment.

Most of the data such as AssignmentID, StudentID and AssignmentDate will be automatically validated by the computer because they will be of a preset type, e.g. Autonumber or Date.

It will not be possible to enter a mark for a student who has not been recorded in the database.

In this section you should discuss which database program you are going to use and the reasons for your choice. The reason may simply be that only one database is available to you.

You need to include details of what data is needed and how it will be collected. Mention how the data will be input to the system.

Validation and verification should be given mention in this section.

Part Two - Analyse

Access 2

You need to show how the data flows through the system. This is best done using Data Flow Diagrams (DFDs). Your teacher should show you how to produce some of these for your project.

Data Flow

At the beginning of the term, Mrs Knight will enter the details of all the students in each class. The details will be sorted by class and surname and stored in the Student table in the database.

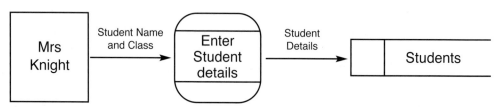

When Mrs Knight sets a new assignment, she enters the details including the title, date set, type of assignment and the maximum mark.

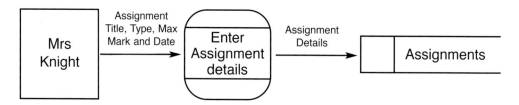

Having entered the student and assignment details, Mrs Knight will enter the individual marks for each assignment as it is completed. Percentage grades are calculated from these marks which will then form the basis for the school reports.

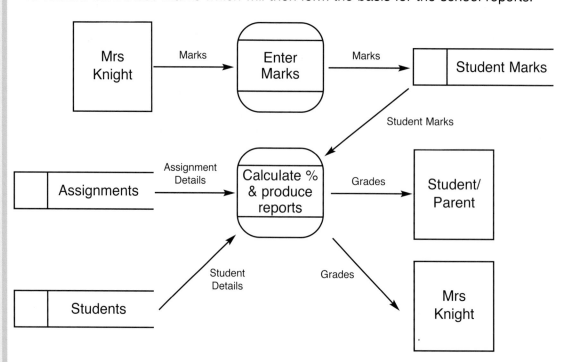

Data Manipulation

The tables required in the system will be Student, Assignment and StudentMark. The individual fields in each table will be as follows:

STUDENT [StudentID, Surname, FirstName, Class]
ASSIGNMENT [AssignmentID, Description, Type, Date, MaxMark]
STUDENTMARK [StudentID, AssignmentID, Mark]

Two reports need to be produced. To produce the report for individual grades, a query will be run to combine data from the three tables. The user will be able to specify the student name and the query will calculate the percentage grade for each assignment. This query will be the source of the individual grade report. The report will find the average mark for the student using the summary function which is part of the Report Wizard

A second report will print the grades for a particular class for a given assignment. The user is asked to enter the assignment code and class name.

Output

The two reports should be viewable on-screen with an option to print them. Reports such as the individual's grades and the class lists of grades for a particular assignment will need to be printed when Mrs Knight goes to parents' evenings. At other times, she may need information such as whether a particular student has passed an assignment. She can view this on-screen.

The reports will group and sort some of the information to make it easier to understand.

Backup / Security Strategy

The computer file containing the final system must be backed up onto floppy disk once a week or whenever a large amount of data is input to the system. This copy should be kept at a different location from the computer in case there is a fire, theft or flood.

There should be some password security on the computer so that students cannot access information not relevant to them. Access has a function to password-protect an application so this should not be a problem. Mrs Knight needs to remember to regularly change her password in case a student finds it out. She should also not write her password down anywhere as this could be an easy way for a student to gain access to the system.

Part Three - Design

Initial Designs

Form Design

There will be 3 forms for data entry.

frmStudent

This form will be used for entering student details for each class taught. My initial design is shown below:

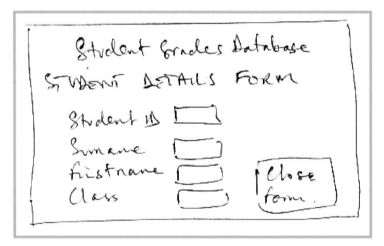

Initial design for frmStudent

frmAssignment

This form will be used for entering details of each assignment, exam, test or homework task before the marks are entered.

frmMarks

This form will be used to input each student's mark for a particular assignment.

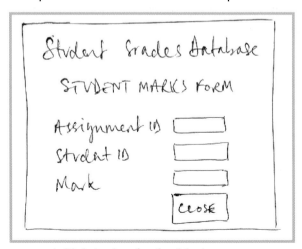

Initial design for frmMarks

Report Design

There will be 2 reports. These can either be printed or viewed on-screen.

rptIndividualGrade

This report will come from a query which combines data from all 3 tables. The user will be able to enter the student's surname, first name and class and the report will show all the grades achieved. It also shows the average percentage grade achieved for each of the different assignment types and an overall percentage. The initial design is shown below:

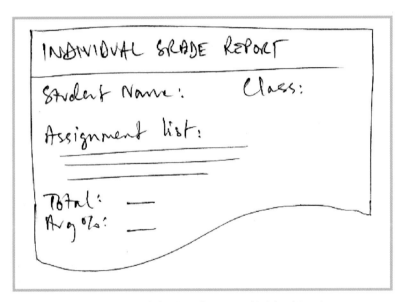

Initial design for rptIndividualGrade

rptClassGrades

This report will show, for each student of a class, the mark and percentage achieved for a particular assignment. The average mark for the class will also be given at the bottom of the report.

Some preliminary designs for the input forms and reports are required at this stage. The user can then use these to judge their suitability for solving the problem.

The report design for rptClassGrades has been left out of this book. It would need to be included in your project.

Menu Design

The menu structure for this system will look like this:

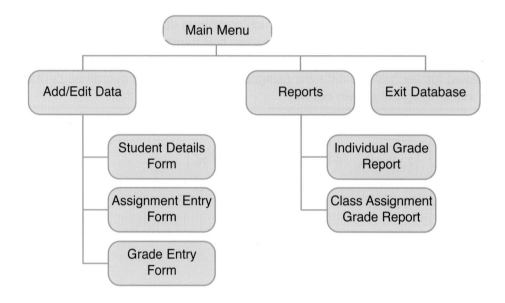

Make sure that you show how the different forms and reports will be linked together. Usually a menu system is made to do this.

Some of the latest version of MS Word have a function to design menu trees like this.

User Feedback on Initial Designs

The initial designs were shown to the Geography teacher for her feedback and approval. Mrs Knight had the following comments and suggestions:

"I have looked at your designs very carefully and they appear to fit my needs. I did however think of one or two little things that you could perhaps change.

1. The assignment types need to include 'Project' in addition to 'Homework', 'Test' and 'Exam'. It would also be very convenient to be able to select this from a list rather than having to type it in each time.

2. Regarding the data entry form for adding pupils' grades, it would be very inconvenient to have to enter each pupil's grade separately. Would it be possible to change this so that I can enter the assignment details once and simply fill in the list of marks for every student in a class on the same form?

3. The Individual Grade report is fine but sometimes I need one of these for every pupil in a class for events such as parents' evenings. Would it be possible to print out an individual report for every pupil in a class without having to enter their names and surnames individually?"

Final Design

Table Design

Three tables are required in this system. They are related as follows:

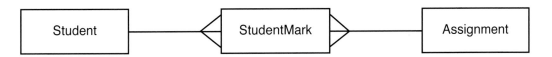

The tables are defined as follows:

tblStudent

Field Name	Data Type	Description/Validation
StudentID	AutoNumber	Unique Primary Key
Surname	Text (20)	
FirstName	Text (15)	
Class	Text (3)	

tblAssignment

Field Name	Data Type	Description/Validation
AssignmentID	AutoNumber	Unique Primary Key
Description	Text (50)	
AssignmentType	Text (15)	Chosen from list
AssignmentDate	Date/Time	Default to today's date
MaxMark	Integer	>0

tblStudentMark

Field Name	Data Type	Description/Validation
StudentID	Long Integer	Must exist on tblStudent
AssignmentID	Long Integer	Must exist on tblAssignment
Mark	Integer	>=0, default to 0

Form Design

The form designs were amended in accordance with Mrs Knight's suggestions and the final designs are shown below. The marks will entered in a subform which is part of the assignment form. A separate form for entering marks is now superfluous.

There is only one form sketched here. Final designs for each of your forms should be included.

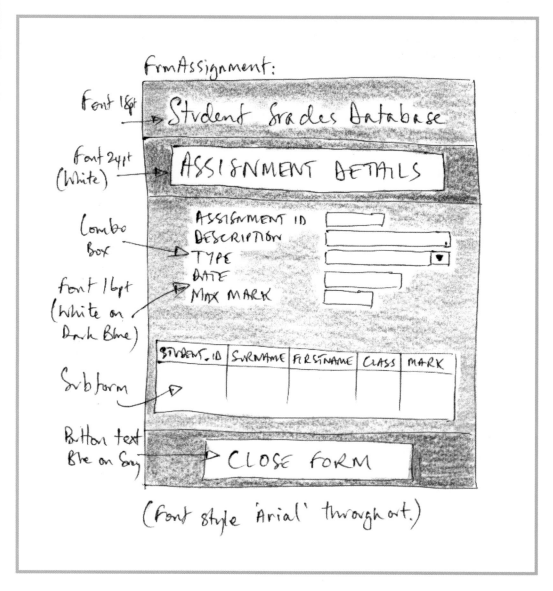

Final design for frmAssignment

Part Three - Design

Query Design

I will need to create 3 different queries. These will form the sources for my reports.

qryIndividualGrade

This query will combine data from all 3 tables. Using all of the fields from these tables, it will ask the user to specify a particular pupil's first name, surname and class. This will then be used to find this pupil's record and display all the grades for the assignments that they have completed. It will also create a new field to calculate the percentage grade for each assignment. It calculates the percentage grade from the mark and the Maximum mark. This is entered as a new field named **Percent**.

e.g. **Percent: [Mark]/[MaxMark]*100**

The criteria allow the user to enter the Surname, First Name and Class for an individual student.

e.g. **[Enter Surname:]**

This query will be used as the source for **rptIndividualGrades**.

qryClassAssignmentGrade

This query will also combine data from all 3 tables. It will ask the user to specify an assignment ID and a class. This will then display a list of pupils in a particular class and the mark they each got for a particular assignment.

qryClassIndividualGrade

This query will be very similar to **qryIndividualGrade** but will only request a class to be entered, rather than the names as well.

> Try to explain how each query will work and what it needs to do.

Report Design

The reports will be the same as in the initial design with the addition of a new one to display the list of assignments and grades for every pupil in a particular class. The **qryClassIndividualGrade** will form the information source for the report. The report design will be identical to the report for individual pupils' grades but will have a page break added to print each pupil's results on a separate page.

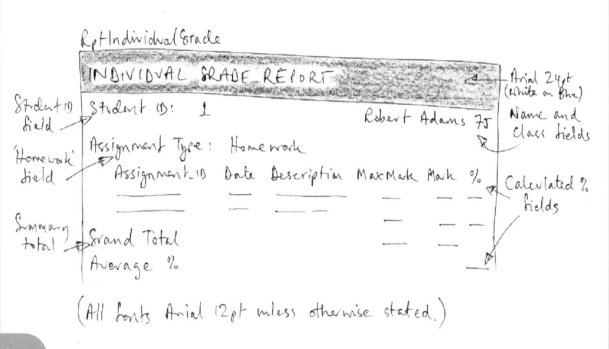

Final design for rptIndividualGrade

There is only one report sketched here. Final designs for each of your reports should be included.

Revised Menu Design

The menu needs to include the extra report and take into account that assignments and grades can now be entered on the same form.

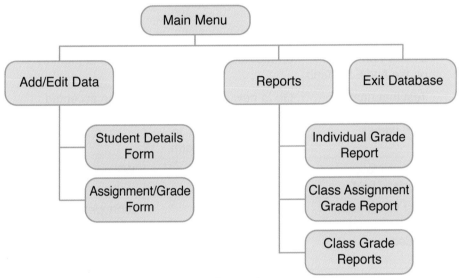

Breakdown of solution into sub-tasks

The implementation of the final design needs to be broken down into more manageable sub-tasks.

1. Create the three tables and define the specified default values and validations.
2. Create the relationships between the tables.
3. Create the data entry form for adding students.
4. Create the data entry form with subform for adding assignments and grades.
5. Create the three queries.
6. Create the three reports.
7. Create the menu.

Test plan

A test plan needs to be devised to make sure that the system does exactly what it is supposed to do. Valid, invalid and extreme data has been used in the tests.

Choose your tests carefully. For these projects, it is much better to thoroughly test part of the system than to inadequately test all parts of the system.

An Access project will require more tests than, say, a PowerPoint or Publisher project.

Test	Purpose of test	Test data	Expected result
1	Test password protection.	Enter 'Grades' for password.	'Grades' accepted and system loads.
2	Test Add/Edit button on main menu.	Click Add/Edit data button.	The Add/Edit Data menu opens.
3	Test the Student Details Form button on the Add/Edit Menu.	Click the button on the Add/Edit Menu.	The Student Details Form opens at the first record.
4	Test that name field can handle long names.	Go to new record enter 'Christopher Bennett-Matthews' in Student Details Form.	Name accepted.
5	Test validation on class field.	Enter 4-digit class code '11GG'	Will not be accepted.
6	Test that a valid record can be added.	Enter 7J for class and press Enter.	tblStudent updated with new record 'Christoper Bennett-Matthews'.
7	Test the Close Form button.	Click the Close Form button.	The Student Details form closes.
8	Test the Assignment/Grade Entry button on the Add/Edit Data menu.	Click the Assignment/Grade Entry menu button.	The Assignment/Grade Entry menu appears.
9	Test to add minimum value of max mark in new assignment.	Enter 'Weather Patterns' as a new 'Project' with a MaxMark of 0.	Value should be rejected. Change MaxMark to 50.
10	Test that student mark cannot be less than 0 for assignment.	Enter mark of -1 Weather Patterns Project for 7J Christoper Bennett-Matthews.	Value rejected. Change to 35.
11	Test to enter a second and third assignment mark for Bennett-Matthews.	Enter mark of 15 (out of 20) for European Capitals homework and 38 (out of 50) for Semi-permeable rocks homework for Bennett-Matthews of 7J.	Grades entered successfully.

Test	Purpose of test	Test data	Expected result
12	Test individual grade report for Bennett-Matthews.	View Individual Grade Report on-screen for Bennett-Matthews, 7J.	Weather pattern project, European capitals homework and Semi-permeable rocks homework grades show.
13	Test that grades are totalled for each assignment.	Add grade totals together manually and compare with computer result.	Total grades for homework should be 53 and for projects should be 35. Grand total should be 88.
14	Test calculated fields on individual grade report.	Manually calculate the average percentage grade and compare with computer result.	Average percentage should be 73.3.
15	Print individual grade report.	Click the Print button and close the report.	Report prints and report screen closes.
16	Test to view Class grade report.	Click Class Assignment Grade Report button and enter 7J as the class and AssignmentID 1.	Report displays on the screen
17	Test calculated fields in class assignment grade report.	Top three percentages should read 60, 35 and 75.	Percentages calculated correctly.
18	Test to view Class grade report.	Click the Class grade report button. Enter 7J for class.	Report for 7J displays on screen.
19	Test that each student has their details on a separate page of the Class grade report.	Scroll through the pages to check each student's details are printed on separate pages.	Each student has their grades printed on separate pages.
20	Exit database.	Click the Exit Grades System button on the main menu.	Database closes.

Part Four - Implement

Finished Design

Evidence that the finished design has been implemented can be seen in the test results section.

Test Results

Now that the system has been created, the test plan devised in the design section can be implemented. Reference to the test plan should be made when looking at the results below.

Test 1: Test password protection

You will find many errors in your system as you develop and test it. Any errors which are thrown up by the test plan should be documented and discussed.

Remember that a successful test is one which reveals an error. It is extremely unlikely - and not even desirable - that your system will work perfectly first time as you work through the test plan. If it does, you need to think of some more demanding tests!

The main menu was displayed after a correct password was entered.

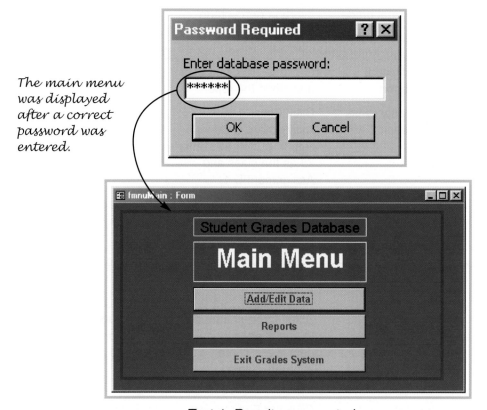

Test 1: Result as expected

The password was requested and accepted when the database loaded to display the Main Menu.

Test 2: Test Add/Edit button on main menu

The Add/Edit Data menu opened as expected when the button on the Main Menu was clicked.

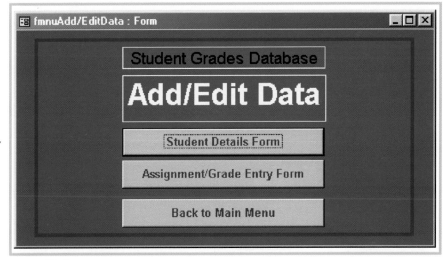

Test 2: Result as expected

Test 3: Test the Student Details Form button on the Add/Edit Data menu

Test 4: Test that the name field can handle long names

The Student Details form opened when the button on the Add/Edit menu was pressed and 'Christopher Bennett-Matthews' was accepted in the name fields.

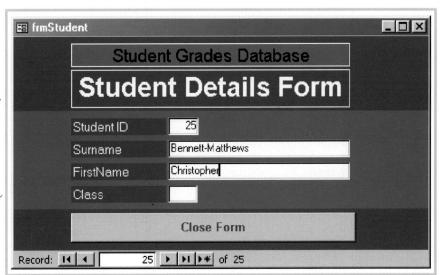

Tests 3 & 4: Results as expected

Test 5: Test validation on class field

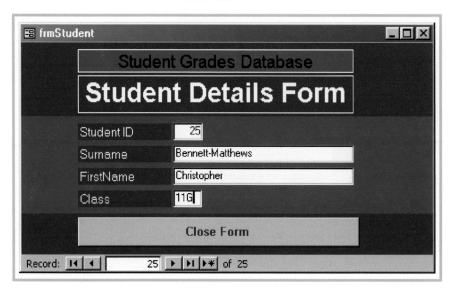

The Class field would not accept '11GG' and beeped to signify an error. Only a maximum of 3 characters was accepted.

Test 5: Result as expected

Test 6: Test to check that a valid record can be added

	StudentID	Surname	FirstName	Class
+	1	Adams	Robert	7J
+	2	Alcock	Gavin	7J
+	3	Berry	Christopher	7J
+	4	Boucher	Sarah	7J
+	5	Catchpole	Davina	7J
+	6	Jee	Sally	7J
+	7	Marriott	Geoffrey	7J
+	8	Nazir	Abdul	7J
+	9	Ahmed	Jamilla	9L
+	10	Chester-Flatt	Jonathan	9L
+	11	Harral	Peter	9L
+	12	Parish	Tracey	9L
+	13	Staunton	Sean	9L
+	14	Wozniak	Viktor	9L
+	15	Bentley	Jane	10A
+	16	Bentley	Melanie	10A
+	17	Eastman	Bert	10A
+	18	Elliot	Joanne	10A
+	19	Elliot	Neil	10A
+	20	Ramkumar	Serena	10A
+	21	Fairchild	Jacob	7J
+	23	Deal	Christopher	10A
+	24	Chrissy	Reeves	10A
+	25	Bennett-Matthews	Christopher	7J
*	(AutoNumber)			

The new record was inserted as number 25 into the end of the student table.

Test 6: Result as expected

Test 7: Test the Close Form button on the Student Details form.

This test worked as expected, closing the Student Details form and redisplaying the Add/Edit data menu.

Test 8: Test the Assignment/Grade Entry button on the Add/Edit Data menu.

This test worked as expected, displaying the Assignment/Grade Entry form.

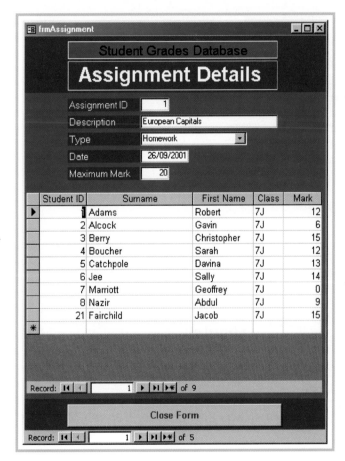

Test 8: Result as expected

Test 9: Test to add below minimum value to Max Mark field in new assignment

An error message appeared when a maximum mark of less than 1 was entered.

Test 9: Result as expected

Test 10: Test that student mark cannot be less than 0 for an assignment.

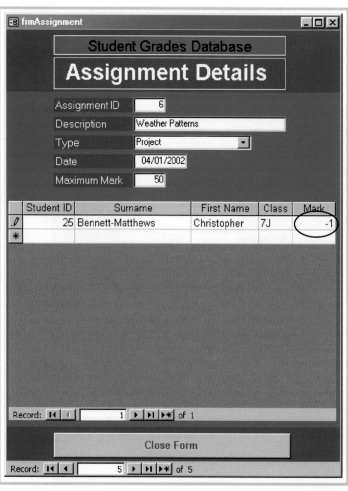

This test should have given an error saying that a mark of less than 0 was not allowed to be entered. The validation rule for this field needs to be corrected.

Test 10: A mark of -1 was accepted for Bennett-Matthews' project

Test 11: Test to enter a second and third mark for Bennett-Matthews.

This test worked as expected and Bennett-Matthews' grades were stored.

Test 12: Test Individual Grade Report for Bennett-Matthews of class 7J

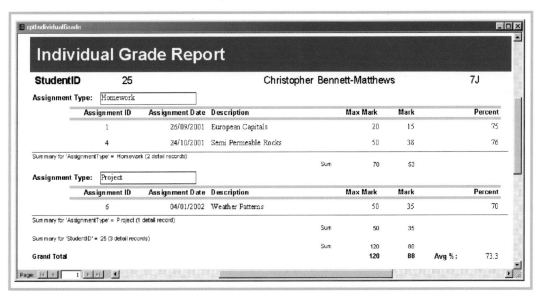

Test 12: Results as expected

The three assignments and their relevant grades were displayed in the Individual Grade Report for Christopher Bennett-Matthews.

Test 13: Test that grades are totalled for each assignment

Total for homework grades is 53 out of 70 and for projects is 35 out of 70. This was as expected. See printout in test 15.

Test 14: Test calculated fields on Individual Grade Report

Calculated fields show percentages of 75, 76 and 70 for each project as expected. The overall average percentage is 73.3 which is also correct. See printout in test 15.

Test 15: Print Individual Grade Report

Always include actual printouts of any reports and annotate them to highlight errors or tests that you have carried out.

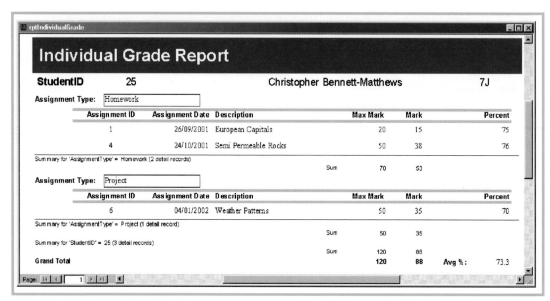

Test 15: Result as expected

The report printed as expected.

Test 16: Test to view Class Assignment Grade Report

Class Assignment Grade Report

Class 7J	Assignment ID	1 European Capitals		Homework	6/09/2001	Max Mark:	20

StudentID	Surname	FirstName	Mark	Percent
1	Adams	Robert	12	60
2	Alcock	Gavin	6	30
25	Bennett-Matthews	Christopher	15	75
3	Berry	Christopher	15	75
4	Boucher	Sarah	12	60
5	Catchpole	Davina	13	65
21	Fairchild	Jacob	15	75
6	Jee	Sally	14	70
7	Marriott	Geoffrey	0	0
8	Nazir	Abdul	9	45

Friday, February 22, 2002 — Page 1 of 1

Test 16: Result as expected

The report displayed on-screen and was printed to make sure that it would come out OK on paper.

Test 17: Test calculated fields in Class Assignment Grade Report
The top three percentages were manually calculated and matched those shown in the report in test 16.

Test 18: Test to view class grade report

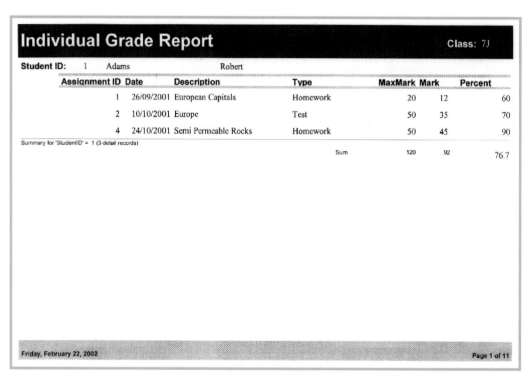

Individual Grade Report   Class: 7J

Student ID: 1   Adams   Robert

Assignment ID	Date	Description	Type	MaxMark	Mark	Percent
1	26/09/2001	European Capitals	Homework	20	12	60
2	10/10/2001	Europe	Test	50	35	70
4	24/10/2001	Semi Permeable Rocks	Homework	50	45	90

Summary for 'StudentID' = 1 (3 detail records)

Sum   120   92   76.7

Friday, February 22, 2002   Page 1 of 11

Test 18: Results as expected

The test was to make sure that the report would display on the screen. A printout was made to make sure that it also printed well. Only the page for Robert Adams is shown.

Test 19: Test that each student has their details on a separate page of the Class Grade Report

This test worked as expected. The 1st page of the report is shown in test 18 and the others each displayed the details of one student. This shows that the page break was put in the right place.

Test 20: The database closed.

Error correction

There was only one test that revealed an error had been made in development. This was the validation rule in test 10 to make sure that an assignment grade could not be less than 0. The validation was added to the assignment table and the test re-run. The following error message was displayed when a grade of -1 was entered.

This is where you need to document the results of the tests that needed to be re-run after corrections had been made to the system.

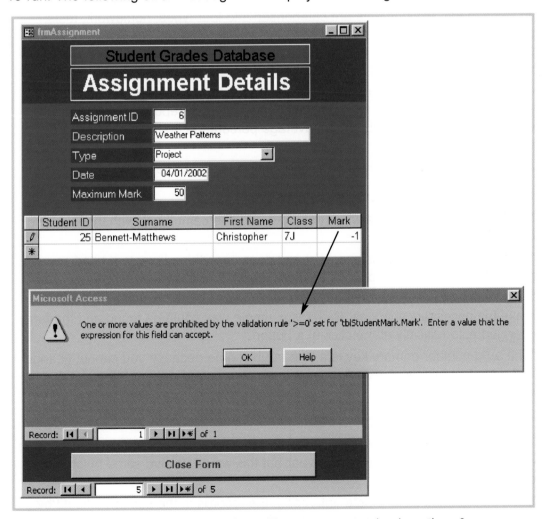

Error message: Validation will not accept grades less than 0

Part Five - Evaluate

Evaluation of Initial Objectives

When the database first loads up, a password is requested. The database window is then displayed and the main menu has to be clicked to start using the actual system. It would be better if this happened automatically.

The system then displays an uncomplicated main menu for the database. This is supported by two further menus which allow the user to either add information or print reports.

All pupil names are stored in alphabetical order which makes it easy for Mrs Knight to compare to her own manual register.

Adding pupil records, assignments or grades into the database is very easy with the aid of data input forms. It takes only a few seconds to enter a pupil's mark for an assignment. Assignments are categorised into four types: homework, tests, projects and exams. This should cover any assignment that Mrs Knight intends to set.

There are three reports. These show a particular student's grades for all the assignments they have done, all the pupil grades for a particular assignment and all the assignment grades for a particular class. In each report, grades are expressed as a percentage and an average percentage grade is given where appropriate.

All the original user objectives have been fulfilled very successfully.

User Feedback on Solution

Mrs Knight was given the system to try out and she came back with the following comments:

"I think that the database is excellent and does everything I wanted. I had some problem with the password since I did not realise it was case-sensitive."

"I did think that next year, once form 7J becomes 8J, that it would be difficult to make the necessary changes. Perhaps a simple way could be found and the forms changed automatically at the click of a button."

"The auto-number primary key is a little troublesome because you cannot change it. If a student joins a class late, they will not be grouped with the others in that class."

Further Ideas for Improvements

The system could be developed to incorporate a button to update each of the form numbers at the beginning of a new year but this would involve some much more complicated design.

In the Assignment Details data entry form, the records in the subform should be sorted in name order rather than StudentID order. This would not be difficult.

> Make sure that you refer back to your original user requirements in the Identify section when you write up your evaluation. You will need to show that you have achieved the objectives, and give reasons if you did not achieve any of them.

> Have at least 2 ideas for further improvement.

Tips for Implementation

This chapter will show you how to build the database using MS Access. Some basic knowledge of this software is assumed.

Creating the database tables

The first step in implementing any database is to create the tables.

▶ Load Microsoft Access and select **Blank Database**.

Creating tblStudent

▶ Click the **Tables** tab and then double-click **Create table in Design view**.

▶ Enter the field names for **tblStudent** as specified in the Design section of the sample project.

▶ Enter any descriptions and the correct field lengths for the **Surname**, **Firstname** and **Class**.

▶ Make **StudentID** the primary key by selecting the row and clicking the **Primary Key** button on the Table Design toolbar. ───────────

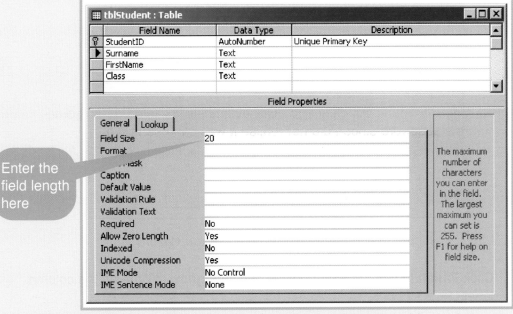

Figure 2.1: Creating a table in Design View

▶ Save and close the table, naming it **tblStudent**.

Creating tblAssignment

▶ Create **tblAssignment** in the same way.

This table has a validation on the **MaxMark** field.

▶ Click in the **MaxMark** row and enter *>0* in the **Validation Rule** box under **Field Properties**.

▶ In the **Data Type** column for **AssignmentType**, select **Lookup Wizard...** This is going to display a list of the various assignment options in the data entry form for this table, saving the user from having to type it in each time.

▶ In the **Lookup Wizard** window, select **I will type in the values that I want** and click **Next**.

▶ Type in *Homework*, *Project*, *Test* and *Exam* and click **Next**.

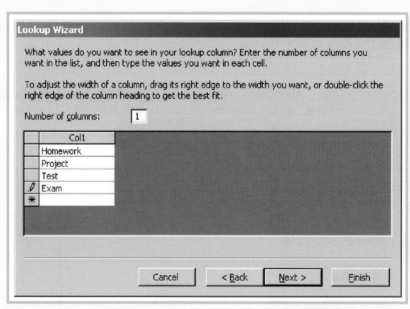

Figure 2.2: Entering values in a Lookup Wizard

▶ Click **Finish** to confirm your choices and **AssignmentType** as the column label.

▶ Select the **AssignmentDate** field and click **Default Value** in the **Field Properties** list.

▶ Enter *=Date()*. This will cause the current date to be automatically entered. The user can change this if required.

Tips for Implementation

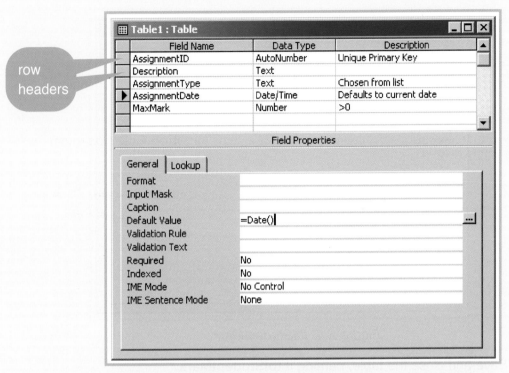

Figure 2.3: Setting the date field to current date by default

● Make **AssignmentID** the **Primary Key**.

● Save and close the table, naming it **tblAssignment**.

Creating tblStudentMark

This table will link the other two tables together. The primary key will consist of the two fields **StudentID** and **AssignmentID**.

● Click the **Table** tab and then double-click **Create table in Design view**.

● Enter the field names for **tblStudentMark** as specified in the Design section of the sample project.

● Enter the correct field sizes and any descriptions for **StudentID**, **AssignmentID** and **Mark**. Note that **StudentID** and **AssignmentID** *must* be Long Integer to link to the AutoNumber fields in the other two tables.

● Select the **StudentID** field by clicking in the row header. Keep your finger on the **Ctrl** key while you click in the **AssignmentID** row header. With both fields selected, click the **Primary Key** button on the toolbar.

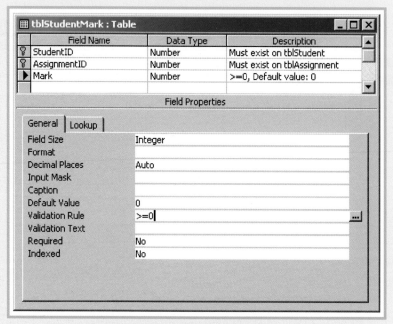

Figure 2.4: tblStudentMark

▶ Save and close the table, naming it **tblStudentMark**.

Defining relationships between tables

▶ With all the tables closed, click **Tools**, **Relationships...** on the main menu.

▶ Add the tables, **tblStudent**, **tblStudentMark** and **tblAssignment** in that order, and click **Close**. The tables appear in the Relationships window; if you have added them in a different order, drag them until they appear as in Figure 2.5.

▶ Create a one-to-many relationship between **tblStudent** and **tblStudentMark** by dragging **StudentID** from **tblStudent** onto **StudentID** in **tblStudentMark**.

Note: Always drag from the **one** side to the **many** side of the relationship – i.e. **one** student has **many** marks.

▶ Check **Enforce Referential Integrity** to ensure that it is impossible to enter a mark for a non-existent student, and check **Cascade Delete Related Records** to ensure that if you delete a student, all marks relating to that student will automatically be deleted. Click the **Create** button.

▶ Create a one-to-many relationship between **tblAssignment** and **tblStudentMark** by dragging **AssignmentID** from **tblAssignment** onto **AssignmentID** in **tblStudentMark**.

▷ Check **Enforce Referential Integrity** to ensure that it is impossible to enter a mark for a non-existent assignment, and check **Cascade Delete Related Records** to ensure that if you delete an assignment, all marks relating to that assignment will automatically be deleted. Click the **Create** button.

▷ Close the Relationships window, making sure the relationships are saved.

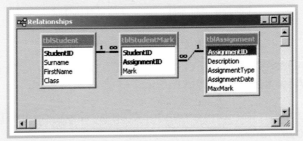

Figure 2.5: Creating the relationships between the three tables

Creating a form for entering student details

▷ From the main database window select **Forms** and double-click **Create form by using wizard**.

▷ Select **Table: tblStudent** from the Tables/Queries list and add all of the Available Fields into the Selected Fields box by clicking the double right-facing arrow.

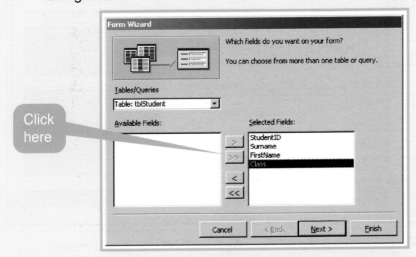

Figure 2.6: Selecting form fields from tblStudent

▷ Click **Next**. Make sure that **Columnar** is selected and click **Next** again.

▷ Select **Standard** and click **Next** once again.

▷ Call the form *frmStudent*. Choose **Open the form to view or enter information** and click **Finish**. It will appear something like the one in Figure 2.7.

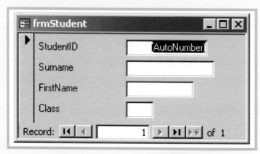

Figure 2.7: frmStudent

▶ Switch to Design View by clicking the **Design View** icon or selecting **View**, **Design View** from the main menu.

▶ Create space in the form's header area by dragging the Detail section header downwards.

▶ Place a label by clicking the **Label** button, and then clicking and dragging where the heading **Student Details Form** is to appear.

▶ Type the text *Student Details Form*. You can adjust its size, justification and font if you wish. The form should look something like the one shown in Figure 2.8.

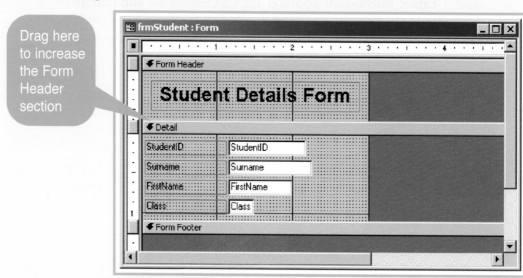

Figure 2.8: Tailoring frmStudent in Design View

▶ Save and close the form.

Creating the student marks form

The second form that we need to create is more complex. Look at the sketch of the form in the Final Design section of the sample project and you will see that it has the details of the assignment in the top half of the form, and then a subform which lists the name and mark of each person in the class.

To get the data into the subform, we first need to combine data from **tblStudent** and **tblStudentMark**. You can do this using a query. This query will then be used as the 'source' for the subform.

Combining data from two tables using a query

- From the database window, click the **Queries** tab and double-click **Create query in Design view**.

- In the Show Table dialogue box, select **tblStudent** and click **Add**.

- Now select **tblStudentMark** and click **Add**.

- Click **Close**.

- Now drag **StudentID** from **tblStudentMark** into the first cell of the query grid. Then drag **Surname**, **Firstname** and class from **tblStudent** onto the grid. Next drag **AssignmentID** and **Mark** from **tblStudentMark** onto the grid. Your query will look like the figure below.

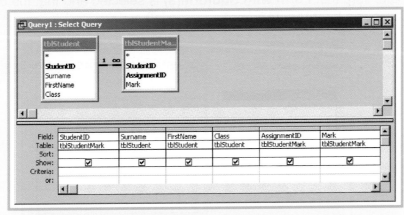

Figure 2.9: The query used to combine data for the subform

- Close the query and save it as **qrySubform**.

Creating a form with a subform

- From the database window click **Forms**, then double-click **Create Form by using wizard**.

- In the next window, select **Table: tblAssignment** in the list of Tables/Queries and add all of the available fields to the Selected Fields box.

- Now select **Query: qrySubform** from the Tables/Queries box and add all the fields to the form except **AssignmentID**. This is not necessary since there is already an **AssignmentID** field added from the Assignment table.

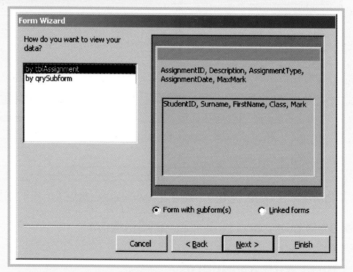

Figure 2.10

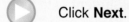 Click **Next**.

Make sure that **Form with Subform(s)** is selected and that the data will be viewed by **tblAssignment**.

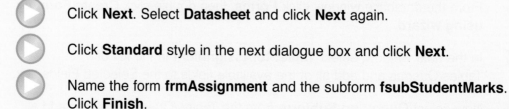

Figure 2.11: Creating a form with subform

Click **Next**. Select **Datasheet** and click **Next** again.

Click **Standard** style in the next dialogue box and click **Next**.

Name the form **frmAssignment** and the subform **fsubStudentMarks**. Click **Finish**.

Your finished form with subform should look something like the one in Figure 2.12.

Tips for Implementation

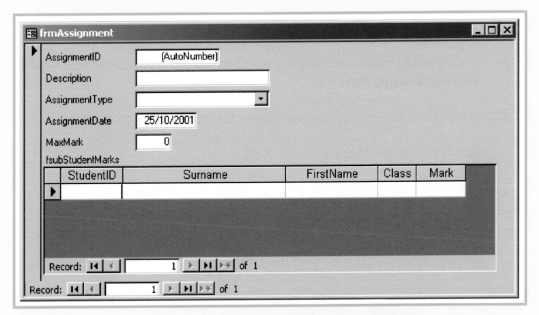

Figure 2.12: The finished form with subform

Adding test data

You will need to start adding some data to the tables. This serves two purposes as it lets you test out your new data entry forms and it gives you some data to use when testing your queries. Try adding invalid or unusual data which tests extreme cases; for example, try adding two students with the same first names and surnames, an assignment ID that already exists or a maximum mark that is less than 1. The latter should give you an error since you put a validation rule to prevent the entry of a maximum mark of less than 0.

You could start to write up a test plan at this stage.

Creating an individual grade report

To do this, another query will need to be created to pick out one particular student specified by the user, and display a list of the assignments they have done, with the relevant grades next to them. Each grade also needs to be expressed as a percentage, with a total average percentage of all their grades for the year so far.

Building the source query

From the database window, click the **Queries** tab and double-click **Create query in Design view**.

In the Show Table dialogue box, select **tblStudent** and click **Add**.

Select **tblStudentMark** and click **Add**.

Now select **tblAssignment** and click **Add**. Click **Close**.

Now drag all of the fields from each table into the query grid except **StudentID** from **tblStudent** and **AssignmentID** from **tblAssignment**. Arrange them as shown in Figure 2.13.

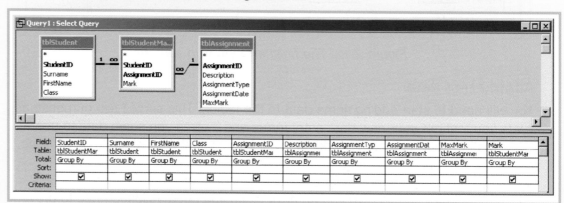

Figure 2.13: The query used to combine data for the report

Adding criteria to a query field

You need to add some criteria to the query so that it will only display information for one student at a time. Since this information must be specified by the user, the query must ask the user what student to search for.

In the Surname field, type *[Surname?]* in the criteria row of the query grid.

This will cause Access to display a pop-up box asking for a surname to be typed in. The name entered will then be used as part of the search criteria in the query.

Because there could easily be two students with the same surname, you need to add a similar line in the **FirstName** field, and likewise, if there are two students with the same first name and surname then the class will need to be entered in the same way too. It is assumed that in this case there will be no identical names in the same class.

Type *[First Name?]* into the **FirstName** criteria row.

▶ Type *[Class?]* into the Class criteria row. See Figure 2.14.

Field:	StudentID	Surname	FirstName	Class	Assignmen	Descript	Assignment1	AssignmentD	MaxMark	Mark	Percent: [Mark]/[MaxMark]*100
Table:	tblStudentMar	tblStudent	tblStudent	tblStudent	tblStudent	tblAssig	tblAssignmei	tblAssignmer	tblAssignm	tblStudentM	
Total:	Group By	Group By	Group By	Group By	Group By	Group B	Group By	Group By	Group By	Group By	Expression
Sort:											
Show:	☑	☑	☑	☑	☑	☑	☑	☑	☑	☑	☑
Criteria:		[Surname?]	[First Name?]	[Class?]							
or:											

Figure 2.14: Adding criteria

Adding a calculated field to a query

As well as showing the actual grade on the report, you need each grade to be expressed as a percentage. You can make a new field which will be named **Percent** to hold the result of the calculation.

▶ Move to the first empty column in the query and type *Percent: [Mark]/[MaxMark]*100* in the Field row. This is the formula which will perform the calculation. **Percent** is the field name – you could have chosen a different name.

▶ Make sure that the Totals are visible by clicking the **Totals** button on the Query Design toolbar.   Σ

▶ Select **Expression** in the **Total:** row from the drop-down menu. See Figure 2.14.

▶ Run your query by clicking the **Run** button on the Query Design toolbar or by selecting **Query**, **Run** on the main menu.   !

▶ You should be asked to enter a surname. Enter the surname for a student you have already entered so you know you should get some results. Click **OK**.

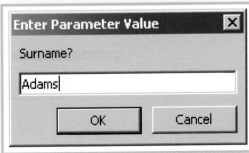

Figure 2.15: Entering 'Adams' as search criteria in the Surname field

Enter a first name and class and click **OK** both times. You should now get a list of assignments for one particular pupil with a percentage grade beside each one. See Figure 2.16.

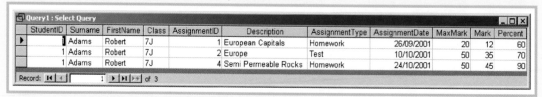

StudentID	Surname	FirstName	Class	AssignmentID	Description	AssignmentType	AssignmentDate	MaxMark	Mark	Percent
1	Adams	Robert	7J	1	European Capitals	Homework	26/09/2001	20	12	60
1	Adams	Robert	7J	2	Europe	Test	10/10/2001	50	35	70
1	Adams	Robert	7J	4	Semi Permeable Rocks	Homework	24/10/2001	50	45	90

Figure 2.16: The finished query showing all assignment grades for Robert Adams of class 7J

> **Save** and close the query. Name it *qryIndividualGrade*.

Using the query to create a report

> In the main Database window click **Reports**.

> Double-click **Create report by using wizard**.

> From the **Tables/Queries** list, select **Query: qryIndividualGrade**.

> Transfer all of the available fields over to the Selected Fields box. See Figure 2.17.

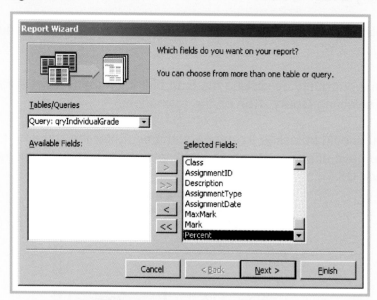

Figure 2.17: Using the report wizard

> Click **Next**.

In the next window select **AssignmentType** and click the right-facing arrow to group the grades by the type of assignment. Click **Next**.

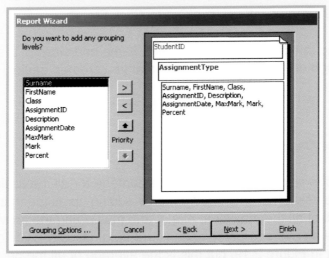

Figure 2.18: Selecting grouping levels for the report

Choose to sort the records by **AssignmentDate** and click on the **Summary Options...** button. This will allow you to add extra information to your report such as running percentages and a total average percentage for the entire year.

Check the **Sum** of **MaxMark** box and the **Sum** of **Mark** box as in Figure 2.19 and click **OK**.

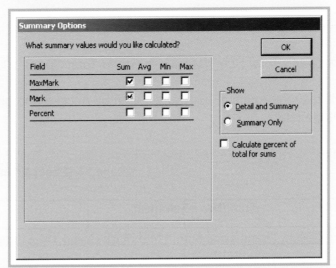

Figure 2.19: Adding summary information to a report

Click **Next**.

Select **Align Left 1** layout and **Landscape** orientation. Click **Next**.

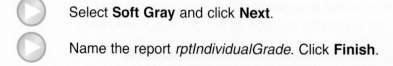

▶ Select **Soft Gray** and click **Next**.

▶ Name the report *rptIndividualGrade*. Click **Finish**.

You will be asked to type in the surname, first name and class of a student since the report is based on, and runs, the query that you created earlier.

Adding a calculated field to a report

▶ Click the **Design View** button.

Ideally you need to calculate the average percentage for all the assignments completed in the year. This should be done by adding up all the marks, dividing them by the total of all the maximum marks and multiplying the answer by 100. (Access will give an average percentage figure automatically if you check the box for **Avg Percent** in Figure 2.19, but this is the average of all the percentages and does not take into account that some assignments may be out of only 10 and others out of 100. Proper testing with a known expected result is crucial to spot this kind of error!)

▶ Click the **Text Box** button on the toolbar and place it in the Grand Total area at the bottom of the report.

▶ Name the text box *Avg %* by typing this in the label section on the left.

▶ Type in the following into the right hand box:

=([Mark Grand Total Sum]/[MaxMark Grand Total Sum])*100

This will take the totals already calculated by Access and give you a percentage total.

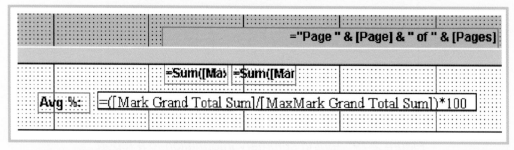

Figure 2.20: The new field at the bottom right of the Individual Grade report

Customising a report

You can further customise your reports by moving the fields around, adjusting their sizes, changing their names and adding a more meaningful title. Colour and formatting can also be added if you so desire.

Individual Grade Report

StudentID	1		Robert Adams			7J

Assignment Type: Homework

Assignment ID	Assignment Date	Description	Max Mark	Mark	Percent
1	26/09/2001	European Capitals	20	12	60
4	24/10/2001	Semi Permeable Rocks	50	45	90

Summary for 'AssignmentType' = Homework (2 detail records)

| | | Sum | 70 | 57 | |

Assignment Type: Test

Assignment ID	Assignment Date	Description	Max Mark	Mark	Percent
2	10/10/2001	Europe	50	35	70

Summary for 'AssignmentType' = Test (1 detail record)

| | Sum | 50 | 35 | |

Summary for 'StudentID' = 1 (3 detail records)

| | Sum | 120 | 92 | |
| Grand Total | | 120 | 92 | Avg %: | 76.7 |

Figure 2.21: The finished individual grade report

Creating the menu system

Look at the Design section of the sample database project to see the menu structure that needs to be created.

▶ In the database window, click the **Forms** tab and select **New**.

▶ In the New Form dialogue box, double-click **Design View** to create a new form without using a wizard. Leave the table or query box blank.

▶ A blank form will appear. Make sure that the **Toolbox** button on the toolbar is selected. Click the **Label** tool and click and drag the cursor on the page to where you want a heading to appear. Type the heading *Add/Edit Data*, and adjust the font, size and position if necessary.

Aa

▶ Make sure that the **Control Wizards** button in the Toolbox is selected. Click the **Command Button** icon, and click and drag the cursor on the form as before.

▶ Select **Form Operations** and **Open Form** from the next window. Click **Next**.

▶ Specify **frmStudent** as the form to be opened. Click **Next**.

▶ Check the option button **Open the form and show all the records**.

Type *Student Details* as button text and click **Next**.

Name the button *OpenfrmStudent*. Click **Finish**.

Place another button on the form to open frmAssignment, in the same way as already described. Your finished form should look something like Figure 2.23.

Click on the small square in the top left hand corner, at the intersection of the ruler lines, using the RIGHT hand mouse button to display a pop-up menu. Select **Properties**.

In the Properties box, change the settings for scroll bars, record selectors, navigation buttons and border style as shown in Figure 2.22.

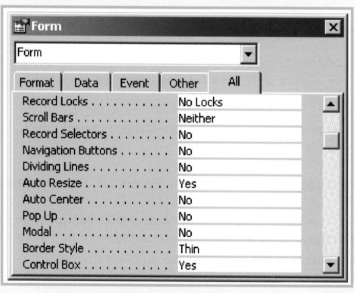

Figure 2.22: Setting the Form properties

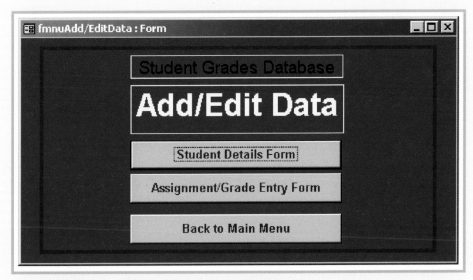

Figure 2.23: The Add/Edit Data menu

Note that a button to return to the main menu still needs to be added to your menu when the main menu screen has been created.

 Save the form as *fmnuAdd/EditData*.

Creating the Reports menu and Main menu

The Reports menu should be created in exactly the same way as the Forms menu. The command buttons perform a **Report Operation** rather than a **Form Operation** as before.

The main menu will use command buttons to open the two menu forms that you have just created. Buttons to go back to the main menu will need to be added to these, as will a button to exit the database on the main menu.

The rest is left to you!

Password protecting the database

The database can have a password put on it using the **Tools**, **Security** options on the main menu. You can do this but it is generally not recommended for a school project since too many students accidentally forget the password. If this happens you will never be able to view your database work and you will have to start the whole project again. So be careful!

Excel

Choosing a Project

Introduction

Spreadsheets are often used for financial purposes but you can also use them wherever calculations need to be performed and data needs to be kept in rows and columns so that it is easy to update and look things up.

Some ideas for extension projects are listed below. Standard projects can use the same ideas with simpler calculations and function.

- A stock control system for a local business
- A mortgage repayment calculator
- A break-even analysis for a proposed business plan
- A scenario analysis for proposals to build a new stand at a football ground
- A record of student grades for different assignments, exams or subjects
- A weights and measures converter
- A budget and booking system for a school play or gig

Ideally you need to demonstrate some of the more advanced functions of Excel in order to obtain the top grades. You will not be assessed on your mathematical ability.

Standard	Extension
Enter text and numeric data	Multiple sheets with automatic transfer of data
Use of formulae	Complex formulae (eg If...)
Multiple sheets	LookUp tables
Printing	Macros
Generate graphs	

Poor Projects

Make sure that your spreadsheet project has enough scope to use the more advanced features of Excel such as VLOOKUP, IF statements, macros and multiple sheets. A project consisting of just one sheet with a few simple formulae to calculate sums and averages will not get you many marks.

On the other hand, there is no need to include a lot of complicated maths. This is unnecessary to convince an examiner that you deserve a top grade.

You need to make sure that whatever project you undertake, there is sufficient information available to complete it.

Checklist for Excel Project

Number	Section	Documentation	Done
1	**Title page**	**Student name, title of project and type of software**	
2	**Identify (5 marks)**	**Section title**	
3		Background detail, identifying the user	
4		Statement of the problem	
5		Manual solution considered	
6		Two alternative software solutions considered	
7		Proposed solution justified	
8		At least 3 quantitative objectives identified	
9	**Analyse (9 marks)**	**Section title**	
10		Appropriate hardware identified	
11		Appropriate software identified	
12		Data required and method of collection explained	
13		Data input explained with details of validation	
14		Data flow diagrams with explanations of what happens to the data between input and output	
15		Alternative methods of output considered with reference to the project (e.g. screen, printer, speakers)	
16		Choice of output method justified	
17		Backup strategy identified	
18		Security strategy (e.g. password) explained	
19	**Design (9 marks)**	**Section title**	
20		Initial designs of worksheets sketched out	
21		Written explanation of initial designs	
22		User feedback on initial designs (comments, letter or questionnaire results)	
23		Final designs drawn up taking user comments into account	
24		Subtasks identified	
25		Test plan of at least 10 tests and expected results	
26	**Implement (12 marks)**	**Section Title**	
27		Brief description of how the design was implemented, explaining any changes that had to be made to the design	
28		Printouts of any reports, with screenshots of each worksheet showing formulae	
29		Evidence that each test in the test plan was carried out, comparing actual results with expected results	
30		When errors occurred, explain how they were corrected	
31	**Evaluate (5 marks)**	**Section Title**	
32		Each original objective fully evaluated. Comment on how well the objectives are fulfilled	
33		A critical comment on anything that you think could be improved	
34		User feedback in the form of a letter or questionnaire. User comment should be critical and relevant	
35		Evidence that you understand the user's comments by making suggestions for future improvements	

GCSE ICT Project

MS Excel

Mobile Phone
Tariff Selector

A.Student

Part One - Identify

Statement of the problem

Mr Sparkes is the owner of a small, but very busy, independent mobile phone shop. It is located in the centre of Ipswich and new and old customers are constantly popping in with questions. The most common question is "Which tariff is the best for me?"

Mr Sparkes cannot always answer this sort of question very easily because it is hard to look at all of the available tariffs on each network and be able to take the customer's circumstances into account.

Currently, a shop assistant has to work out manually, using a calculator and a pen and paper, a rough estimate of which would be the best tariff. Frequently they don't bother and make a guess based on experience. They are often not up-to-date with the latest tariffs and so the customer does not get the best deal.

Each network publishes its tariffs and associated costs in a slightly different way and talk plans on different networks are not comparable with each other. For example, one network offers their cheapest tariff for £15 with 1500 free minutes and calls charged at 35p/min, whereas another will offer it for £12 with 600 free minutes and call charges at only 10p.

What Mr Sparkes really needs is a system that will let the customer or sales assistant input their personal phone usage and calculate which tariff, on which network, is best for them.

Having a system such as this will allow Mr Sparkes more time to talk to other customers and increase the quality of service he provides.

Consideration of Alternative Solutions

There are a variety of different ways in which this problem could be solved.

The first method, to calculate everything by hand, is the method being used and it needs to be replaced by a better system.

A set of well-thought-out printed tables could help in finding the best tariff but this would end up being a large catalogue of many pages and would still be very inconvenient to make any sort of instant comparisons from and equally difficult to keep up-to-date.

A computer could be used to store the information about costs for each network. The user (a sales assistant) could type in the customer's average monthly usage and the computer would display the most economical tariff.

If a computer is used, there are several alternative solutions:

- A special program could be written to do this. This would be very time-consuming and I do not have the skills to do it.

- A database package could be used. The tariffs could be stored but databases are not well-suited to applications that require a lot of calculations.

> Make sure that you include the name of the user, a description of the system they currently use and the problems they have in using that system.

> It is sometimes useful to include examples from the current situation to help describe the problems associated with it.

> It is important to try and think of at least one manual method of solving the problem and another software solution in addition to the spreadsheet solution you will inevitably be using for this project.

95

Full justification of the final solution is required.

- A spreadsheet could be used. Separate worksheets can be used for the user to enter their monthly usage, and to store the tariffs for each network and calculate the cheapest tariff.

Chosen solution

I am going to use a spreadsheet because:

- The tariffs for each network can be looked up on the Internet and easily updated every week in the spreadsheet. In a manual solution, tables would have to be reprinted.
- A nice-looking user interface will be easily achieved, and will have its own worksheet.
- A simple button running a macro can display the best network and tariff for a particular user's requirements.
- It will provide a much more accurate answer to a user's problem than the current manual method. Obviously any recommendation will be based on the user's ability to accurately estimate their usage.

User Requirements

The user has quite a clear idea in his head about what the system should be like and has specified the following requirements:

1. The system must have a friendly user interface with a clear screen form for entering customer details.
2. The system must allow the user to enter their peak and off-peak usage, as well as the average number of text messages they send each month.
3. The system must cater for all four mobile phone networks and their tariffs.
4. The system must calculate the cheapest possible tariff of the four networks.
5. The system must give a clear answer to the user, stating the network, the talk plan and how much it would cost.
6. The system should find an answer within 3 seconds.
7. The system must be robust enough to handle even the largest usage figures.
8. The system should not involve any additional hardware or software costs.

User requirements should be measurably achievable.

Part Two - Analyse

Part Two - Analyse

Appropriate Software and Hardware

Since a spreadsheet has been chosen as the most effective solution, which spreadsheet package to use must now be considered.

Lotus 1-2-3 is a popular spreadsheet program and would be quite suitable for solving such a problem. Unfortunately I am not familiar enough with the software to create the system and nor is the shop owner, Mr Sparkes, should he need to update it.

Microsoft Excel (Version XP) is the other alternative that I have. This is the best known package and would be perfect since I do know how to use it. Mr Sparkes is also capable of using it on a very basic level. This would make it easier for him to update the system when tariffs change in the future. Mr Sparkes has also already got MS Office (which includes MS Excel) installed on his computer and would not have to buy any extra software.

MS Excel is the software that I will use as it does not cost anything extra since Mr Sparkes already has it and our knowledge of how to use it is much better than Lotus 1-2-3.

The hardware required will consist of a basic processor, (calculations in Excel do not require great processor speed), monitor, mouse and keyboard. The system will be used by a sales assistant using the computer already in the shop. The monitor can swivel so that customers can see for themselves the results of the search.

Data Required

The data required to build this system will be the tariff information from each of the four different mobile phone networks. When the system is used, the customer will need to supply:

- Their average monthly peak usage
- Their average monthly off-peak usage
- The average monthly number of text messages they send

Specifically, the information required for each network is:

- A list of the different talk plans
- Their monthly charges
- The amount of free talk time given
- Call charges – Peak and Off peak for each tariff
- Individual text message charges

> Discuss using other spreadsheet packages, then give reasons for your choice.

> Specify which version of the software you will be using.

> Think carefully about all the data that you will need and specify where it will come from.

Data Collection

> It is a good idea to include any research you have done - this could include actual leaflets.

The tariff information can be found on leaflets in Mr Sparkes's shop or on the Internet. It is important that the most up-to-date tariffs are used so as to give the most accurate results. It would be good idea to collect the data from both sources mentioned and check that they agree.

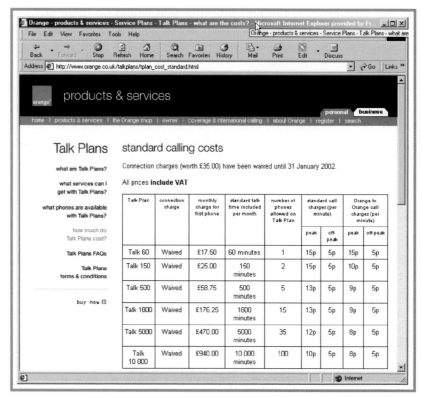

A mobile phone network website showing tariff information

The user will need to get their input data from their mobile phone bill if they currently have a mobile phone, from their land line bill if they only have a land line or from friends who are likely to have a similar usage to themselves.

Data Input

> State how the data will be input into the system and what validation you will need to perform.

Once the information has been collected I will key it into the spreadsheet straight from the leaflets. All updates made to the system when tariffs change will be keyed in by Mr Sparkes. The sales assistants will key in the usage figures for the customers when the system is being used.

The initial data entry and any updates will be verified by visually checking it once it has been entered. The customer's usage figures will need to be automatically validated so the system will not accept negative usage and will only accept figures up to 20,000 minutes used in a month (equivalent to about half the total number of minutes in a month) and 1,500 text messages (an allowance of 50 per day).

Part Two - Analyse

Data Flow

Updating tariff information

Mr Sparkes updates the tariffs whenever the networks change them. The new tariff information replaces the old information in the spreadsheet.

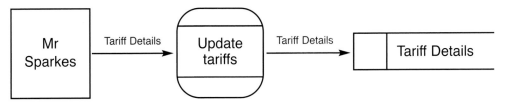

You will need to show the data flow through the system using a data flow diagram. Ask your teacher for help if you need it!

Dealing with customer enquiries

A sales assistant enters the customer's average monthly usage into the system and the details of the best tariff are given to the customer, though sometimes via the sales assistant.

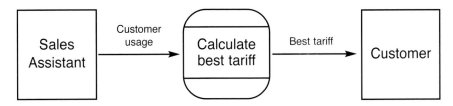

Data Manipulation

The raw tariff information will need to be keyed into the spreadsheet. Formulae will be entered into the spreadsheet to find the best tariff.

The data is manipulated as follows:

- User enters estimated peak and off-peak minutes, and number of text messages.
- Formulae are used to calculate the monthly cost for each network.
- These costs are copied to a Tariffs worksheet and sorted into ascending order.
- The first on the list (i.e. the cheapest) is displayed on the user's screen.

What happens to the data once it has been entered? Is it changed in any way before it is output?

Output

A button will run a macro to calculate the best tariff for the customer and display it on-screen with the respective network and talk plan. A printout of the customer's results could be given to them but since it is just a single piece of information, it is expected that they can remember it or jot it down on a piece of paper. The aim will be to sell them a phone there and then and not to encourage them to walk out of the shop with a printout to think about it.

Describe whether the output is hard copy or screen-based.

Backup / Security Strategy

The computer file containing the final system must be backed up onto floppy disk. This copy should be kept at a different location from the computer in case there is a fire, theft or flood at the shop premises. A backup copy needs to be made each time the system is updated.

There should be some password security on the computer so that people using the system cannot change any of the formulae. This can be done by protecting the worksheet so that nothing can be changed except the values that the customer will input. If anyone attempts to make a change or to unprotect the worksheet, Excel will ask for a password.

The password should be at least six characters and preferably not a common word such as 'Sparkes' or 'Mobile' that is easily guessed and nor should it be written down. It should be not too obvious but something Mr Sparkes can memorise.

Be sure to mention the frequency of backups, and what medium is used.

Mention the precautions needed to protect the secrecy of a password.

Part Three - Design

Part Three - Design

Initial Designs

An initial design for the system was drawn up as follows:

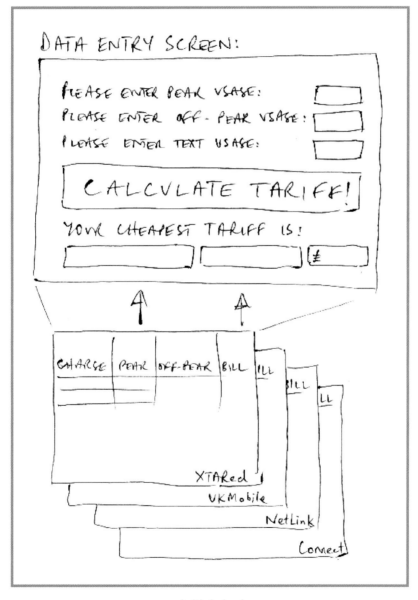

You must handraw these designs before you get to the computer. They do not need to be in any detail.

Initial design

The spreadsheet will calculate the cheapest tariff based on the figures that the user inputs on the entry form. The tariff information from each network is stored on a separate sheet. Each of these sheets contains tables of formulae which will calculate the tariff for each Talk Plan. The system will then sort the table of figures by 'Total Bill' and perform a lookup operation to post the result back to the entry form for the user to see.

This operation will be done at the click of a button using a recorded macro assigned to it.

User Feedback on Initial Designs

Mr Sparkes said that he liked having the talk plans for each different network on a separate sheet. This, he said, would provide better information should a customer insist on a particular network because, for example, their friends are also on it.

He also said that he thought it best not to ask the customer for their calls to other mobiles and frequency of calls to the answer phone because they will not be able to accurately estimate this and it just makes the system more confusing and complicated than it needs to be. The changes he wanted, he made himself to the initial design shown.

The more user feedback you get, the more likely you will end up with a satisfactory project.

Part Three - Design

Final Design

Final design: Data Entry sheet

You can make a copy of a blank spreadsheet layout at the back of this book and use it for your designs.

Remember: your final designs need to be detailed enough for someone else who knows Excel to be able to implement your system the way you intended it.

	A	B	C	D	E	F	G	H
1	XTARed							
2								
3	Talk Plan	Monthly Charge	Free Minutes	Peak Call Charges	Off Peak Call Charges	Text Message charges		
4	Talk 60							
5	Talk 150	(Data to be entered from Internet						
6	Talk 500	or leaflet)						
7	Talk 1800							
8	Talk 5000							
9	Talk 10000							
10								
11								
12		Chargeable Peak	Free minutes unused	Chargeable Off-Peak	Total Peak Charge	Total Off Peak Charge	Total Bill	
13	Talk Plan							
14	Talk 60	(see Design Section for formulae)						
15	Talk 150							
16	Talk 500							
17	Talk 1800							
18	Talk 5000							
19	Talk 10000							
20								
21			= MIN (G14:G19)					
22	Best tariff	=VLOOKUP (B22, TariffList, 3)		(N.B. TariffList is a named range on TariffTable)				

SHEET NAME : XTARed   Design Sheet 2

Final design: The XTARed phone company sheet (Design Sheet 2)

This is how each of the individual phone company sheets will look. The other network sheets will differ only in the talk plan details and the colour scheme. UKMobile, NetLink and Connect will have blue, green and orange respectively, as their colour schemes.

	A	B	C	D	E
1	COST	OPERATOR	TALK PLAN		
2	=XTARed! Q14	XTARed	Talk60		
3					
4					
5					
6					
7	(costs for all operators, all talk plans				
8	ie monthly bills for a given estimated usage)				
9					
10	This table is a named range "TariffList".				
11					
12	When the user presses the button on the Data Entry				
13	worksheet, the table will be sorted by COST.				
14					
15					
16					

SHEET NAME : Tariff Table   Design sheet 3

Final design: The Tariff Table sheet (Design Sheet 3)

Breakdown of solution into sub-tasks

The implementation of the final design will need to be broken down into more manageable sub-tasks:

1. Create data entry form. Add validations to each cell where the user can enter data.
2. Set up row and column headings and enter data for each of the tariffs on each network. Name worksheet tabs and cells.
3. Enter the formulae to calculate the total bill for each of the tariffs.
4. Make final sheet listing each tariff and corresponding monthly bill.
5. Sort by monthly bill and post the details of the cheapest tariff back to the data entry screen.
6. Add a button on the data entry screen which runs a macro to perform task 5.
7. Smarten up the data entry screen.
8. Protect all cells except those which require input from the customer, and add a password.

Task 1: Create Data Entry form (Design Sheet 1)

A title will need to go at the top of the page. This will be followed by three headings and space to input a value after them:

Please Enter your Average Peak Minutes Used:	####
Please Enter your Average Off-Peak Minutes Used:	####
Please Enter your Average No. of Text Messages Used:	####

I will need to give names to each of the cells containing input values. This will make them easier to refer to in my formulae. They will be called PeakUsage, OffPeakUsage and TextUsage respectively.

The validation rules will be:

PeakUsage must be between 0 and 20000

OffPeakUsage must be between 0 and 20000

TextUsage must be between 0 and 1500.

Part Three - Design

Task 2-3: Set up row and column headings, enter data and formulae (Design Sheet 2)

The worksheets for each network will be similar but formulae may be in different cells because of varying numbers of different tariffs.

The left hand cells in each row will hold all of the talk plan names.

Cell Reference in Design Sheet 2	Column Heading	Cell Value or Pseudocode Formula
B4-B9	Monthly Charge	Value
C4-C9	Free Minutes	Value
D4-D9	Peak Call Charges	Value
F4-F9	Text Message Charges	Value
B14-B19	Chargeable Peak	=IF(PeakUsage>Free Minutes, 0)
C14-C19	Free Minutes Unused	=IF(Chargeable Peak Minutes =0), Free Minutes - PeakUsage, 0)
D14-D19	Chargeable Off-Peak Minutes	=IF(OffPeakUsage<FreeMinutesUnused, 0, OffPeakUsage-FreeMinutesUnused)
E14-E19	Total Peak Cost	=ChargeablePeakMinutes *PeakCall Charges
F14-F19	Total Off-Peak Cost	=ChargeableOffPeakMinutes *OffPeakCharges
G14-G19	Total Bill	=TotalPeakCost+TotalOffPeakCost +MonthlyCharge+(TextMessageCharges* TextUsage)

The formulae in the table above can be applied to the information entered in the tables to calculate the total bill for each talk plan on one network.

This table and formulae can then be copied across to other worksheets to calculate talk plans for the remaining networks.

Task 4: Make final sheet listing each tariff and corresponding monthly bill (Design Sheet 3)

This sheet is a list of all the talk plans for each company, together with the total monthly bill for the user's estimated usage. Formulae are used only in column A, to pick up the calculated total bill from the relevant sheet.

Task 5-6: Sort by monthly bill and post the details of the cheapest tariff back to the data entry screen

A button will need to be put onto the Data Entry screen so the user can click it to find out the cheapest tariff of the four networks. The button will act as a trigger to tell Excel to sort the Tariff table (Design Sheet 3) by total bill and then copy the cheapest total onto the Data Entry screen.

The corresponding network and talk plan details will then be copied over to the Data Entry screen from row 2 of the sorted table to display the cheapest figure and the name of the Network and Talk Plan.

A macro will then be recorded to perform these steps. The macro will be assigned to the button on the Data Entry screen.

Task 8: Protect all cells except those which require input from the customer, and add a password

As a final touch, the spreadsheet will be protected with the exception of the three cells in which the user will need to enter their estimated usage. This means that the user cannot change anything else without a password.

> It is especially important to do some manual calculations to compare with those done using formulae. Include tests to test each validation rule in your system.

Test Plan

A test plan needs to be devised to make sure that the system does exactly what it is supposed to do. Where possible I have used extreme data to test all scenarios to the maximum.

Test	Purpose of test	Test data	Expected result
1	Test validations for peak minutes.	Enter -1, then 20001 for peak usage. Then enter *abc*	Values not accepted - error messages displayed.
2	Test validations for off-peak minutes.	Enter -1, then 20001 for off-peak usage. Then enter *abc*	Values not accepted - error messages displayed.
3	Test validations for text usage.	Enter -1 and then 1501 for text usage. Then enter *abc*	Values not accepted - error messages displayed.
4	Test for peak usage more than free minutes.	Input data 100, 200, 50.	XTARRed Talk 60 will show 40 chargeable peak minutes and 200 chargeable off-peak minutes. Total bill calculated as £37.75.

Test	Purpose of test	Test data	Expected result
5	Test for peak usage less than free minutes.	Input data: 50, 200, 50.	On UKMobile, no chargeable peak and 150 chargeable off-peak minutes. Total bill for Net 100 £47.50.
6	Test that Tariff table correctly sorted.	Input data: 550, 2000, 500.	Table sorted into ascending order of total bill and minimum value returned to Data Entry screen.
7	Test maximum allowable values.	Input data: 20000, 20000, 1500.	Total bill £2194 on NetLink 720.
8	Test minimum allowable values.	Input data: 0, 0, 0.	The total bill for each network will be the same as the monthly charge for each tariff. The cheapest bill is with Connect at £14.99.
9	Test a mixture of max and min values.	Input data: 0, 20000, 0.	NetLink will be cheapest bill.
10	Test time taken to calculate tariff after entering data.	Input data: 100, 100, 100.	It should take less than three seconds to return the cheapest tariff.
11	Test to see if cells outside of cells G4 to G6 can be edited.	Input 123 in cell G11 of data entry sheet and cell B14 of XTARed worksheet.	No edits accepted. Error message displayed requesting password.

Part Four - Implement

Finished Design

The finished design has been implemented in Microsoft Excel. A customer can enter their estimated average usage on the data entry screen as shown below. The design has been slightly altered in the final implementation by removing the gridlines.

The data entry screen

In this example, the user has entered 100, 200 and 50 for their estimated average peak, off-peak and text message usage. They then press the **Find the Best Tariff** button and the system returns NetLink 150 on the NetLink network.

The formulae for this screen are shown below.

The data entry screen formulae

It is important to show the formulae you used in your spreadsheet. This is evidence that the system was implemented as intended. You can do this in Excel by selecting **Tools**, **Options** and then checking the **Formulas** box.

The macro attached to the button sorts the tariff table by total bill. The code for this is shown below.

```
MobilePhone.xls - Module1 (Code)

(General)                                SortList

Sub SortList()
'
' SortList Macro
' Macro to sort TariffList by cost in ascending order
'
    Sheets("TariffTable").Select
    Range("A1:C23").Select
    Selection.Sort Key1:=Range("A2"), Order1:=xlAscending, Header:=xlGuess, _
        OrderCustom:=1, MatchCase:=False, Orientation:=xlTopToBottom, _
        DataOption1:=xlSortNormal
    Sheets("DataEntry").Select
End Sub
```

The SortList macro

To view the macro code, click **Tools, Macro, Macros...** from the menu. Select the macro and click **Edit**.

There are four worksheets for each of the mobile networks. The formulae for the first network, XTARed, are shown below.

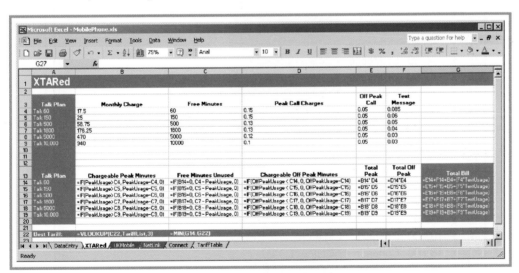

The formulae for the XTARed worksheet

Use a whole page and print out the formulae in your documentation. To display the formulae, click **Tools, Options...** on the menu and select the **Formulas** option from the **View** tab.

The formulae for the other 3 networks are the same.

The final sheet, **TariffTable**, is a list of all the tariffs. When the customer enters their estimated usage, the total bill for each tariff is calculated using the formulae shown above. These figures are copied to **TariffTable** and sorted using the **SortList** macro.

The minimum tariff on the network is calculated using the MIN function and displayed in cell C22. The corresponding Talk Plan name is then displayed next to it, in cell B22. This is calculated using the VLOOKUP function to find the name in the sorted list in the **TariffTable** worksheet.

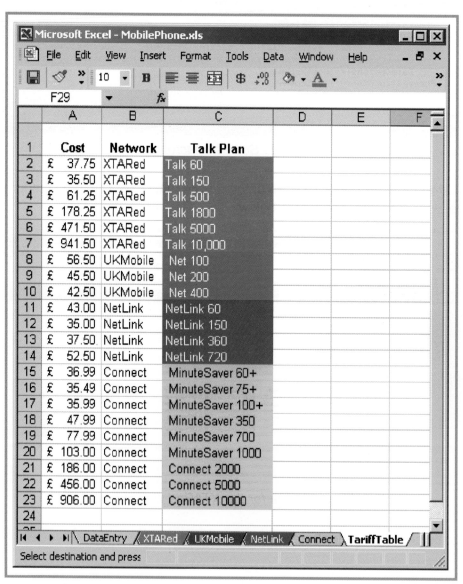

The TariffTable worksheet showing formulae

Diagram showing processes involved

This shows how the system has been implemented.

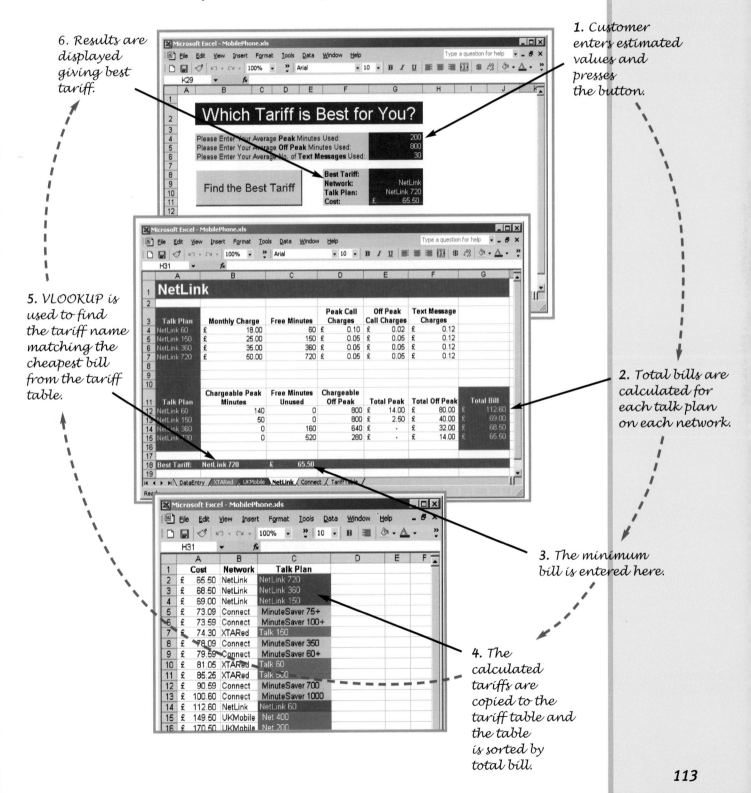

6. Results are displayed giving best tariff.

1. Customer enters estimated values and presses the button.

5. VLOOKUP is used to find the tariff name matching the cheapest bill from the tariff table.

2. Total bills are calculated for each talk plan on each network.

3. The minimum bill is entered here.

4. The calculated tariffs are copied to the tariff table and the table is sorted by total bill.

Test Results

This section shows the results of the test performed following the test plan in the Design section.

Test 1: Test Validations for peak minutes

An invalid value is not accepted, an error message is displayed as expected.

Test 1: Result as expected

The error message was also displayed when *20001* and *abc* were entered.

Test 2: Test Validations for off-peak minutes

An invalid value is not accepted, an error message is displayed as expected.

Test 2: Result as expected

The error message was also displayed when -1 and abc were entered.

Test 3: Test Validations for text message usage

An invalid value is not accepted, an error message is displayed as expected.

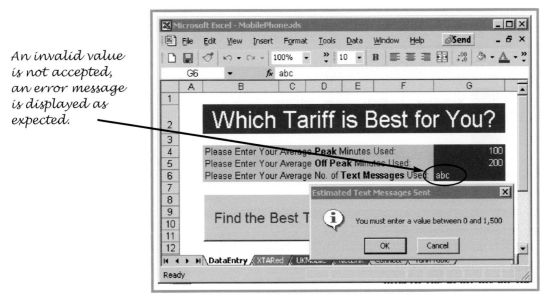

Test 3: Result as expected

The error message was also displayed when -1 and 1501 were entered.

Test 4: Test for Peak Usage > Free Minutes. Input data: 100, 200, 50.

As expected, this network shows 40 chargeable peak minutes, 200 chargeable off-peak minutes and the total bill is £37.75.

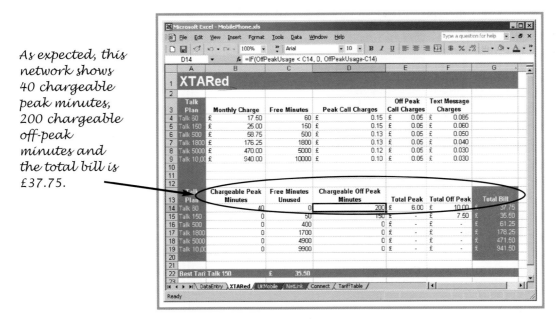

Test 4: Result as expected

Test 5: Test for Peak Usage < Free Minutes. Input data: 50, 200, 50.

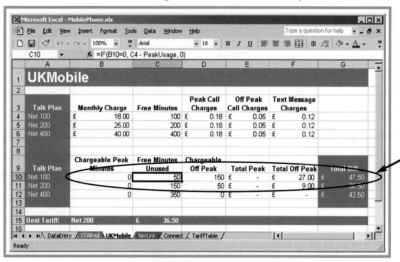

As expected, this network shows 0 chargeable peak minutes, 50 free minutes unused, 150 chargeable off-peak minutes and the total bill is £47.50 for Net 100.

Test 5: Result as expected

Test 6: Test that tariff list is correctly sorted. Input data: 550, 2000, 500.

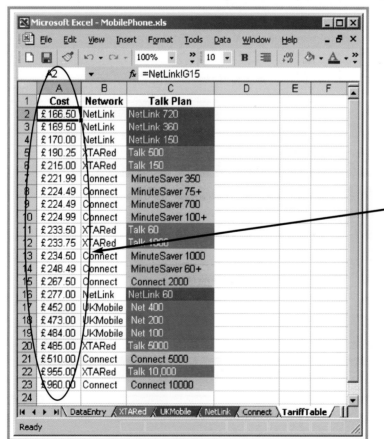

As expected, the macro correctly sorted the table by cost and returned the NetLink 720 plan on the NetLink tariff as the cheapest at £166.50.

Test 6: Result as expected

Test 7: Test maximum allowable values. Input data: 20000, 20000, 1500.

The system handled the large estimates without any problem but the column width for total bill was too narrow to display the large totals. This was then corrected.

The actual cheapest bill was £2089. The error was in the manual calculation I made for the expected result.

Test 7: Total bill column width needed to be adjusted.

Test 8: Test minimum allowable values. Input data: 0, 0, 0.

As expected, the cheapest bill is the one with the cheapest monthly charge. The monthly charges are equal to the total bill amounts.

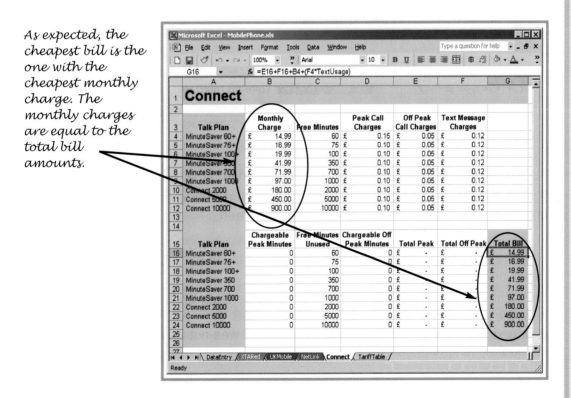

Test 8: Result as expected

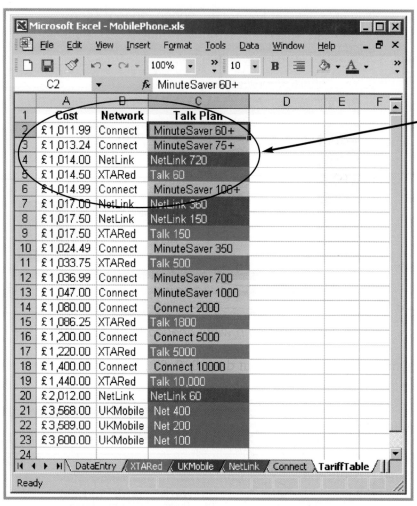

NetLink was not the cheapest bill but this was an error in my calculations for the expected result. The system correctly calculated the cheapest bill at £1011.99 with Connect.

Test 9: Error in manual calculation

Test 10: Test time taken to calculate tariff after entering values.

This test was done using a stopwatch and took less than a second to return the details of the cheapest tariff to the data entry screen.

Test 11: Test to see whether cells other than G4 to G6 can be edited without a password.

This test involved clicking on different cells on the Data Entry worksheet. It was not possible to click in any cell except G4, G5 and G6. Only cells G4 to G6 could be changed and the button still worked. A password was not asked for, as expected – instead, nothing happened.

Part Five - Evaluate

Evaluation of Initial Objectives

The system has a friendly user interface and Mr Sparkes found it extremely easy to use.

A customer or sales assistant can enter their average estimated peak and off-peak usage and the number of text messages they send each month.

The system caters for all four mobile phone networks. However, it does not include all the tariffs for every network because some of the tariffs are calculated in a completely different way and it was beyond the scope of this project to include them. The current tariffs have been entered into the spreadsheets using leaflets and information from the Internet. One problem is that these tariffs will change quite frequently and Mr Sparkes will have to update the data on the spreadsheet. If additional tariffs are added, this may mean some formulae need to be changed. Also, the named range on the tariff table sheet will need to include the new entries.

It calculates the cheapest possible tariff and displays the network, talk plan and cost on the user screen in less than one second.

It handles all valid estimated values and rejects invalid user entries.

User feedback on solution

Mr Sparkes was very pleased with the spreadsheet, however he foresaw some problems in using it as the only means of estimating the best tariff for a customer. For example, several networks give discounted calls to other customers on the same network as the caller. Also, estimates do not take into account calls to other mobiles, which are more expensive than land lines. He agreed that it would have been extremely complicated to include this and since tariffs are constantly changing, it would also be time-consuming to keep up-to-date.

Further suggestions for improvements

The system would be even more useful if it included an easy facility to add more tariffs and update existing tariff information. Some special tariffs that are calculated differently do not fit in with the way in which this system has been designed.

When the user presses the button, the screen flicks briefly onto the tariff table worksheet when it sorts it and then changes back again to the data entry screen. It would be possible to write a macro preventing this so that the tariff table is updated invisibly.

Read through your user requirements and in your evaluation, describe how well each of the objectives has been met.

Don't pretend the system is perfect - you will get credit for being perceptive enough to spot weaknesses which the examiner may also have spotted!

Tips for Implementation

Tips for Implementation

This chapter will show you how to build the Excel project. You will find it useful to implement this project before starting on your own, as you will be learning and practising advanced skills.

Setting up the spreadsheet

We will start by designing the data entry screen as shown in Design Sheet 1. The final screen will look like this:

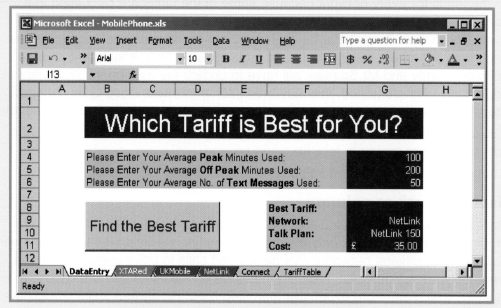

Figure 3.1: The final data entry screen

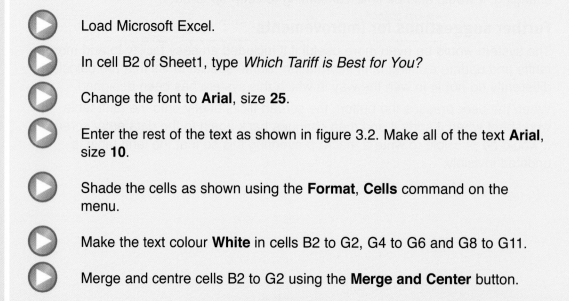

Load Microsoft Excel.

In cell B2 of Sheet1, type *Which Tariff is Best for You?*

Change the font to **Arial**, size **25**.

Enter the rest of the text as shown in figure 3.2. Make all of the text **Arial**, size **10**.

Shade the cells as shown using the **Format**, **Cells** command on the menu.

Make the text colour **White** in cells B2 to G2, G4 to G6 and G8 to G11.

Merge and centre cells B2 to G2 using the **Merge and Center** button.

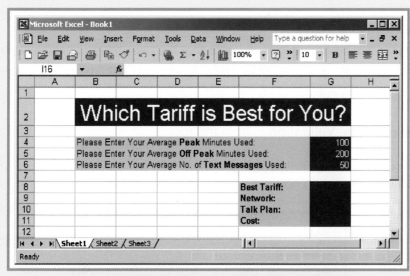

Figure 3.2: Designing the Data Entry screen

The command button will be added later.

Naming Cells

Naming cells makes formulae that reference the cells much easier to understand.

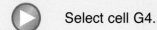 Select cell G4.

From the **Insert** menu, select **Name**, **Define...**

Type the name *PeakUsage* and click **OK**. See figure 3.3.

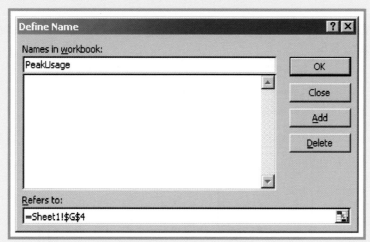

Figure 3.3: Naming a cell

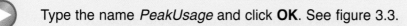 Name cell G5, *OffPeakUsage*.

Name cell G6, *TextUsage*.

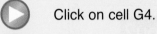
Adding validation rules

Validation rules can be added to make sure that the user enters sensible values for their estimated usage. This is an important part of any project and will earn you marks.

▶ Click on cell G4.

▶ Select **Data**, **Validation…** from the menu.

▶ Make entries as shown in Figure 3.4. This will only allow a whole number between 0 and 20,000 to be entered in this cell.

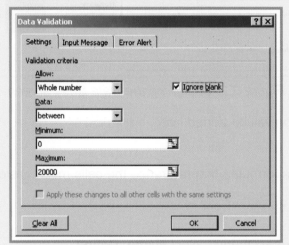

Figure 3.4: Adding a validation rule to a cell

▶ Click on the **Error Alert** tab at the top of the **Data Validation** window.

▶ Choose an **Information** style message and enter the text shown in Figure 3.5.

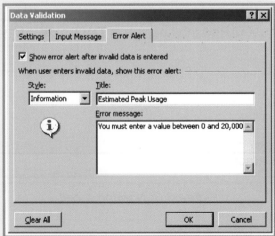

Figure 3.5: Defining an error message

▶ Click **OK**.

▶ Test your validation by entering some invalid numbers and letters.

▶ Add a validation to cell G5. This must also be between 0 and 20,000. A similar error message can be defined.

▶ Add a final validation to cell G6. The average number of text messages sent must be between 0 and 1,500. Add a suitable error message.

▶ Save the spreadsheet as **MobilePhone.xls**.

Adding and naming worksheets

You should name your worksheets so that they are easily identifiable. In Excel 2002 you can also colour the worksheet tabs. This workbook needs 6 worksheets so the first task is to add 3 more.

▶ Select **Sheet3** and choose **Insert**, **Worksheet** from the menu.

This will have put a new worksheet called Sheet4 in front of Sheet3 but this does not matter since you will be renaming them anyway.

▶ Insert another 2 worksheets.

▶ Right-click **Sheet1** and select **Rename** from the shortcut menu.

▶ Rename this sheet *DataEntry* and press **Enter**.

▶ Call the rest of the sheets *XTARed, UKMobile, NetLink, Connect* and *TariffTable*.

▶ Right-click the **XTARed** tab and select **Tab Color...** from the list of options.

▶ Select **Red** from the colour palette and click **OK**.

▶ Colour the other tabs as shown below.

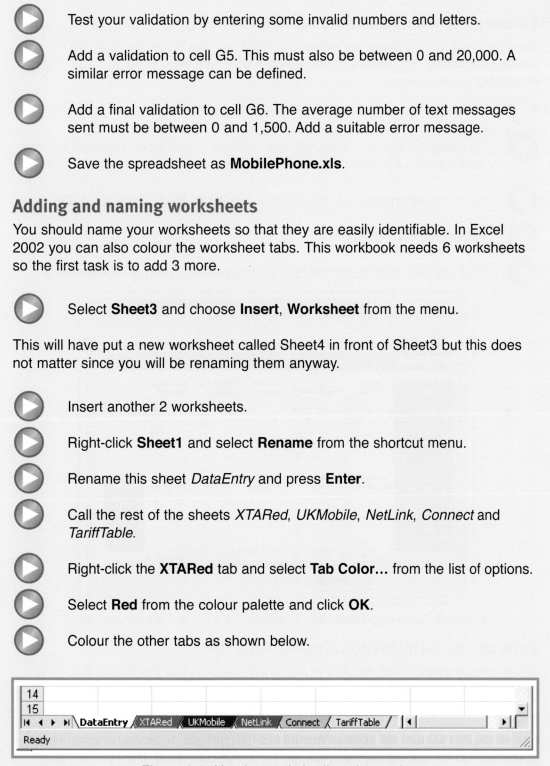

Figure 3.6: Naming and shading sheet tabs

Entering the labels and data for XTARed

We now need to implement the design for XTARed, the first of the four mobile phone companies. You must assume that the data has been collected from the Internet or from leaflets.

▶ Enter the labels and data as shown in Figure 3.7.

▶ To make the column headings wrap around inside a cell, highlight the cell and from the **Format** menu, select **Cells...**

▶ Click the **Alignment** tab and choose the **Wrap Text** option. Click **OK**.

▶ Shade the cells as shown.

▶ You will also need to format the cells containing charges as **Currency**.

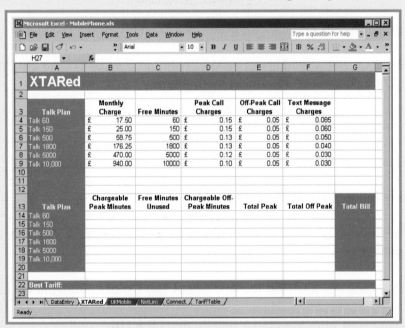

Figure 3.7: Adding the labels and data for XTARed phone company

Entering the formulae to calculate Total Bill

The formulae in the lower half of the sheet will make use of the IF function. The format of the IF function is:

$$=IF(condition, value\ if\ true, value\ if\ false)$$

For example, the number of peak minutes to be charged depends on whether the customer has exceeded the free minutes for a particular tariff. If they have, the number of chargeable minutes will be the total peak minutes used minus the free minutes. If the customer has not used all the free minutes, the chargeable minutes will be zero.

The formula is:

> =IF(PeakUsage>Free Minutes, PeakUsage – Free Minutes, 0)

 In cell B14, enter the formula

> *=IF(PeakUsage>C4, PeakUsage – C4, 0)*

(Recall that **PeakUsage** is the name of the cell on the Data Entry sheet where the user enters their estimated usage).

 Copy it down to cells B15 to B19.

The **Free Minutes Unused** (column C) will be 0 if all the free minutes have been used, otherwise they will be the difference between the free minutes for the tariff and the minutes actually used.

The formula is:

> =IF(Chargeable Peak Minutes=0, Free Minutes - PeakUsage,0)

 In cell C14, enter the formula

> *=IF(B14=0, C4 - PeakUsage, 0)*

 Copy it down to cells C15 to C19.

The formula for **Chargeable Off-Peak Minutes** needs to work out whether the user has enough free minutes left unused to cover their off-peak calls. If they have, they will not be charged for them. If their off-peak usage has exceeded the amount of free minutes unused, then the difference must be calculated. The difference will be the chargeable off-peak minutes.

The formula is:

> =IF(OffPeakUsage < Free Minutes Unused, 0, OffPeakUsage –
> Free Minutes Unused)

 In cell D14, enter the formula

> *=IF(OffPeakUsage < C14, 0, OffPeakUsage –C14)*

 Copy it down to cells D15 to D19.

 In cell E14 enter the formula for Total Peak Charges. This will be

> *=B14* D4*

 Copy it down to cells E15 to E19.

▶ In cell F14 enter the formula for **Total Off-Peak Charges**. This will be:

$$=D14* E4$$

▶ Copy it down to cells F15 to F19.

▶ In cell G14 enter the formula for the total bill. This will be

$$=B4 + E14 + F14 + (TextUsage * F4)$$

▶ Copy it down to cells G15 to G19.

The **XTARed** worksheet should now look like this:

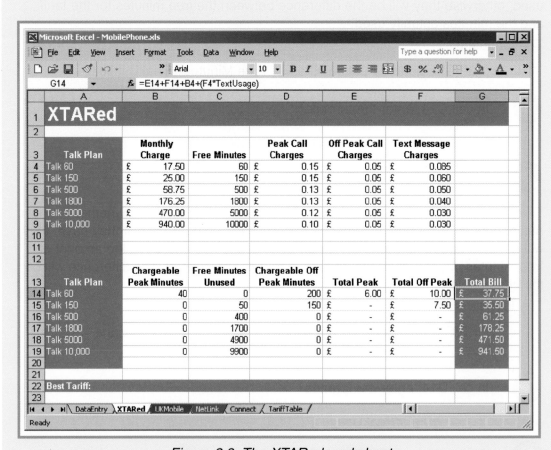

Figure 3.8: The XTARed worksheet

Worksheets for each network

Now the worksheets for the remaining three networks need to be created. These will have their own separate data but use identical formulae to the **XTARed** worksheet.

The **UKMobile** worksheet will look like this:

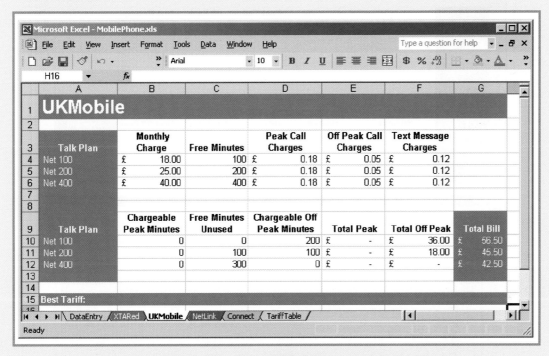

*Figure 3.9: The **UKMobile** worksheet*

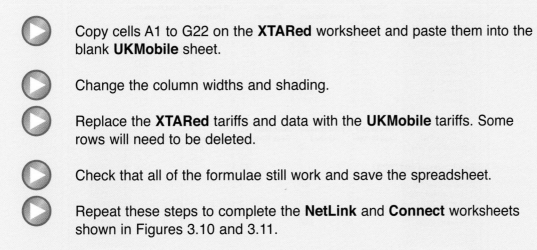

▶ Copy cells A1 to G22 on the **XTARed** worksheet and paste them into the blank **UKMobile** sheet.

▶ Change the column widths and shading.

▶ Replace the **XTARed** tariffs and data with the **UKMobile** tariffs. Some rows will need to be deleted.

▶ Check that all of the formulae still work and save the spreadsheet.

▶ Repeat these steps to complete the **NetLink** and **Connect** worksheets shown in Figures 3.10 and 3.11.

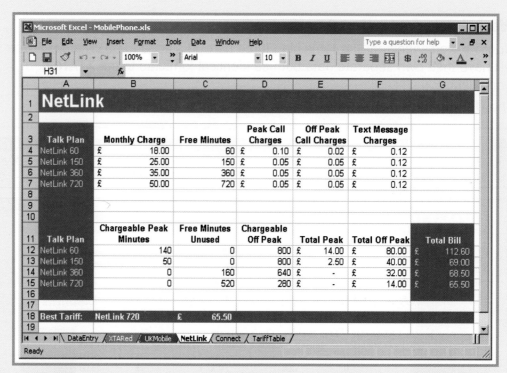

Figure 3.10: The **NetLink** worksheet

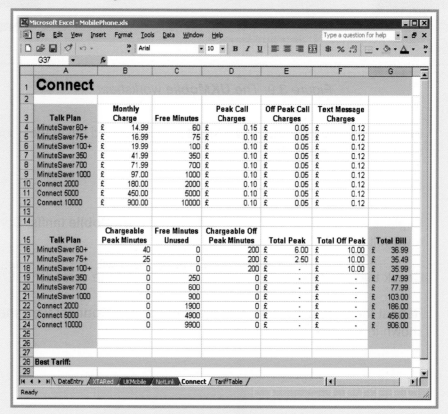

Figure 3.11: The **Connect** worksheet

Finding the cheapest tariff on a particular network

To find the cheapest of a range of different totals for the monthly bill, you will need to use the MIN function. This finds the minimum value in a specified range.

▶ Click the **XTARed** worksheet tab.

▶ Select cell C22.

The formula needs to find the minimum value in the range G14 to G19. These are the figures for the total bill for each tariff.

▶ In cell C22 enter the formula *=MIN(G14:G22)*

▶ Press **Enter**.

▶ The cheapest total bill should appear in C22 as shown in the Figure 3.12. The usage estimates entered in this instance were 100, 200 and 50 for **Peak**, **Off-Peak** and **Text Messages**.

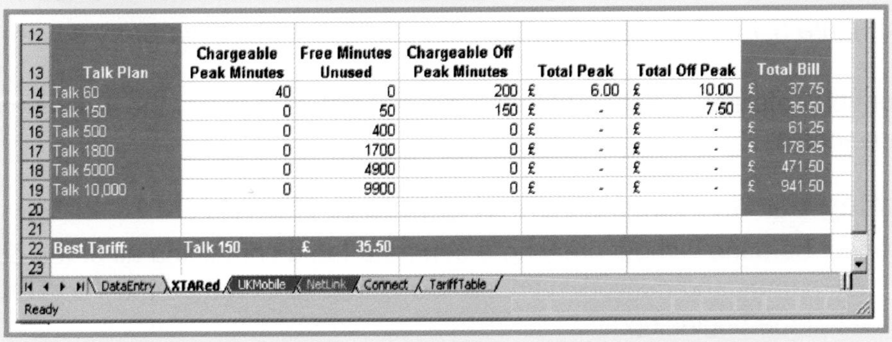

	Talk Plan	Chargeable Peak Minutes	Free Minutes Unused	Chargeable Off Peak Minutes	Total Peak		Total Off Peak		Total Bill	
14	Talk 60	40	0	200	£	6.00	£	10.00	£	37.75
15	Talk 150	0	50	150	£	-	£	7.50	£	35.50
16	Talk 500	0	400	0	£	-	£	-	£	61.25
17	Talk 1800	0	1700	0	£	-	£	-	£	178.25
18	Talk 5000	0	4900	0	£	-	£	-	£	471.50
19	Talk 10,000	0	9900	0	£	-	£	-	£	941.50
20										
21										
22	Best Tariff:	Talk 150	£	35.50						
23										

◄ ► ►│ DataEntry \ XTARed ⁄ UKMobile ⟨ NetLink ⟨ Connect ⟨ TariffTable ⁄

Ready

Figure 3.12: Finding the minimum value within a range

▶ Repeat this for the other 3 networks.

Finding the cheapest tariff of all the networks

The lowest cost of all the networks needs to be found and displayed on the Data Entry screen for the user to see. This is done by inserting a similar formula using the MIN function into the Data Entry screen. The formula will find the minimum of the cheapest tariffs that you just calculated for each individual network.

▶ Select the **DataEntry** screen.

▶ Click in cell G11.

▶ Enter the formula

=MIN(XTARed!C22,UKMobile!C15,NetLink!C18,Connect!C28)

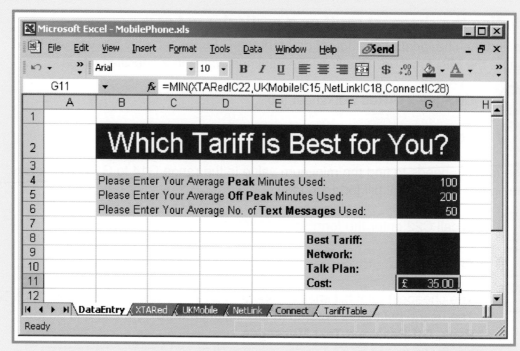

Figure 3.13: Returning the minimum total bill to the Data Entry screen

This formula references each of the minimum tariffs on each of the 4 different network sheets.

Matching the tariff and network names to the lowest total bill

This cannot be done without creating a separate table containing all of the different costs, tariff names and network names. This is why you created the **TariffTable** worksheet at the beginning.

 Click on the **TariffTable** worksheet.

 Add the column headings *Cost*, *Network* and *Talk Plan* in cells A1, B1 and C1.

Now you need to copy the cost figures from the **XTARed** worksheet into the **Cost** column of the Tariff table.

 In cell A2 of **TariffTable**, enter the formula *=XTARed!G14*. This refers to cell G14 of the **XTARed** sheet.

 Copy the formula down to cell to cell A7.

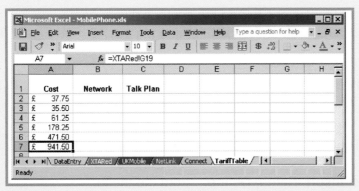

Figure 3.14: Copying values from another worksheet

▶ In cell B2, in the **Network** column, type *XTARed*.

▶ Copy this down to cell B7.

▶ Now click on the **XTARed** worksheet tab.

▶ Highlight cells A14 to A19.

▶ Select **Edit**, **Copy** from the menu.

▶ Click the **TariffTable** sheet tab and click in cell C2.

▶ Select **Edit**, **Paste** from the menu. This will put in each of the talk plan names that correspond to the costs.

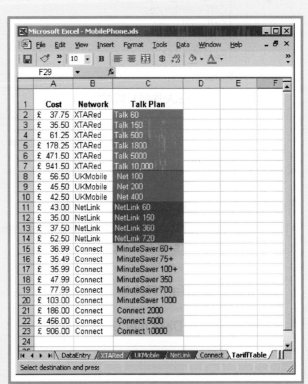

*Figure 3.15:
The TariffTable worksheet*

Repeat these steps to add the costs, network name and talk plan names for each network underneath, starting in cell A8. See Figure 3.15.

Naming a range of cells

To make a range of cells easier to refer to, you can give it a name. In this case you will name the range A1 to C23 in **TariffTable** and call it **TariffList**.

 Highlight cells A1 to C23 of the **TariffTable** worksheet.

 Select **Insert**, **Name**, **Define...** from the menu.

 Type in *TariffList* as the range name.

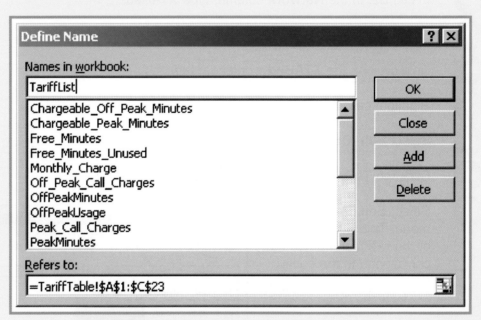

Figure 3.16: Naming a range of cells

 Click **OK**.

Sorting a range of cells

The range **TariffList** needs to be sorted into ascending order by cost so that the lowest cost appears at the top of the table.

 With the **TariffTable** worksheet in view, select cells A1 to C23.

 From the **Data** menu, click **Sort...**

Figure 3.17: Sorting TariffList in ascending order by cost

Make sure that **Cost** is showing in the **Sort by** box and that the **Ascending** option is selected.

Click **OK**.

Now the list is sorted, you know that the network and talk plan that correspond to the cheapest total bill will always be in cells B2 and C2. You can use this to display this information on the **DataEntry** sheet.

Click on the **DataEntry** sheet tab.

In cell G9, enter the formula, *=TariffTable!B2* and press **Enter**.

In cell G10, type *=TariffTable!C2* and press **Enter**.

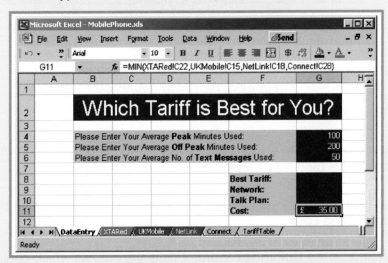

Figure 3.18: The Data Entry screen

The VLOOKUP function

This function is used to find a particular value in the first column of a table and display another value in a different column on the same row in that table.

The format of this function is:

=VLOOKUP(Value to find, Table name or range, Column number)

You need to use this function to display the name of the cheapest tariff at the bottom of the worksheets for each network. You cannot assume that the cheapest tariff for a particular network will always appear at the top of the Tariff table so you need to look it up in the list.

> This is a very useful function and you will earn marks for using it.

 Click on the **XTARed** worksheet tab.

 Select cell B22.

 Click **Insert**, **Function...** from the menu.

 Select the **VLOOKUP** function from the **Lookup & Reference** category.

> The functions are in alphabetical order so it should be at the bottom of the list.

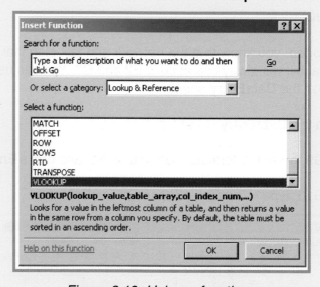

Figure 3.19: Using a function

 Click **OK**.

 Now enter C22 as the **Lookup_value**. (You need to find the value in cell C22 in the TariffList on the TariffTable worksheet.)

 Type in *TariffList* as the **Table_array**. This is where you want to look for the value in C22.

 Enter 3 as the **Col_index_num**. This is the column which contains the value you want to be displayed on the XTARed worksheet.

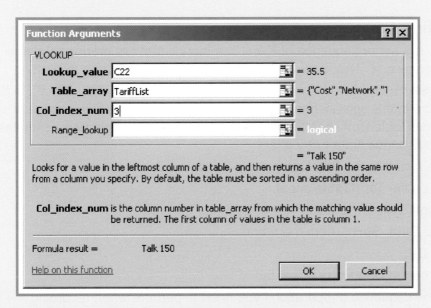

Figure 3.20: The VLOOKUP function

▶ Click **OK**.

▶ Check that you now have the talk plan name displayed in cell C22.

12									
13	**Talk Plan**	**Chargeable Peak Minutes**	**Free Minutes Unused**	**Chargeable Off Peak Minutes**	**Total Peak**		**Total Off Peak**		**Total Bill**
14	Talk 60	40	0	200	£	6.00	£	10.00	£ 37.75
15	Talk 150	0	50	150	£	-	£	7.50	£ 35.50
16	Talk 500	0	400	0	£	-	£	-	£ 61.25
17	Talk 1800	0	1700	0	£	-	£	-	£ 178.25
18	Talk 5000	0	4900	0	£	-	£	-	£ 471.50
19	Talk 10,000	0	9900	0	£	-	£	-	£ 941.50
20									
21									
22	**Best Tariff:**	**Talk 150**	£	35.50					
23									

◄ ◀ ▶ ►\ DataEntry \ **XTARed** ⟋ UKMobile ⟋ NetLink ⟋ Connect ⟋ TariffTable ⟋

Ready

Figure 3.21: The talk plan name is displayed using the VLOOKUP function

▶ Repeat these steps to display the name of the cheapest talk plan at the bottom of the remaining 3 network sheets.

Recording a macro

A macro is a set or sequence of Excel commands that are grouped together and performed as one. This macro will then be assigned to a button to perform all of the commands when the button is pressed. Using a macro can earn you extra marks.

The macro in this spreadsheet needs to sort **TariffList** (this is the range of values on the TariffTable worksheet) after the user has entered some new estimates for their usage on the Data Entry sheet.

1. Make sure that the **DataEntry** sheet is displayed.
2. Click on the **TariffTable** sheet.
3. Highlight cells A1 to C23.
4. Select **Data**, **Sort**… from the menu.
5. Click **OK**.
6. Click on the **DataEntry** sheet tab.

This is the sequence of operations you need to perform when recording the Macro. It is best to practise the sequence of operations once or twice first before recording to make sure you know exactly what you are going to do.

Now you are ready to record.

 Select **Tools**, **Macro**, **Record New Macro…** from the menu.

 Name the macro *SortList*. Type in a description as shown in Figure 3.22.

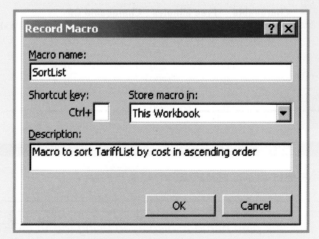

Figure 3.22: Recording a macro

 Click OK.

 Perform steps 1 to 6 above.

 Click the **Stop Recording** button. (This should appear in a small window of its own that floats over the rest of the screen.)

Creating a button

Now you need to add a button to the DataEntry sheet. This will then run the macro when it is clicked.

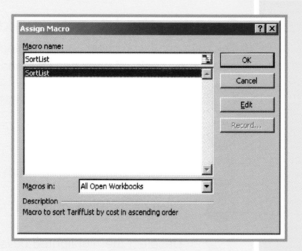

- ▶ Right-click the menu bar and select **Forms** from the shortcut menu. This will display the Forms toolbox.

- ▶ Click the **Button** tool.

- ▶ Now click the **DataEntry** sheet where you would like the button to be placed.

Figure 3.23

- ▶ The Assign Macro window should automatically appear. Select the **SortList** macro that you recorded earlier.

- ▶ Click **OK**.

- ▶ Add some text to the button and change its size and colour if you wish.

- ▶ You can remove the gridlines from the sheet by selecting **Tools**, **Options...** from the menu and deselecting **Gridlines** from the **View** tab.

Figure 3.24: The finished DataEntry sheet

Protecting the data entry worksheet

The data entry worksheet can be protected so that only the cells in which the customer enters their peak, off-peak and text message usage can be changed without a password.

▶ Click on the **DataEntry** sheet tab.

▶ Highlight cells G4 to G6.

▶ Select **Format, Cells...** from the menu.

▶ Click on the **Protection** tab and clear the **Locked** check box.

▶ Deselect the highlighted cells by clicking anywhere on the sheet.

▶ Select **Tools, Protection, Protect Worksheet...** from the menu.

Figure 3.25: Protecting a worksheet

▶ Check the **Select unlocked cells** option and click **OK**.

▶ Try clicking on any of the cells other than G4 to G6. You will find that you are not able to. To remove the protection, select **Tools**, **Protection**, **Unprotect Sheet...**

You could have added a password to unlock the worksheet when you protected it. This option has been left blank in Figure 3.25 as passwords can be difficult to remember.

▶ Experiment using your system with some different estimates for peak, off-peak and text message usage and see what results you get.

Publisher

Choosing a Project

Introduction

First of all, you need to identify a real user. This is quite easy since most of the things commonly produced in DTP packages such as leaflets, brochures, business cards and posters are used widely in schools and businesses. Some good ideas for a project are shown below:

- A sports day leaflet, winner's certificate and entry ticket for the PE department.

- A programme, ticket and poster for a school play organised by the drama department.

- A newsletter for your local youth club or Scout group.

- A letterhead, business card and compliments slip for a parent's workplace or business.

- A menu, wine list and advertisement for a restaurant at a part-time work placement.

You can include up to, say, 3 different related items in your project in order to fully demonstrate your ICT skills. When deciding on what to design, remember that it is only the high level skills that will get the top marks. Some examples of standard and extension problem types are shown below:

Standard	Extension
Entering and editing text	Importing data from another application
Changing font type and size	Image manipulation
Inserting clip art	Text flow between blocks
Page setup	Creating a logo
Columns	
Printing	

Some poor project ideas are:

Designing a poster for an event – this will probably be too simple and will not involve sufficient extension level features of the software to gain a top grade.

Designing a magazine – this is too ambitious a project and far more than necessary. It will take too much time to complete and may end up looking a little ratty towards the end if it is hurriedly finished. A front and back cover with a page of text in the middle would be perfect to demonstrate the skills necessary to get the A grades.

Do not try to make a famous company such as Coca-Cola or Cadbury your 'real user'. It is unlikely that these companies will want to give you their time and it will be difficult to think of any problems they have for which you are able to offer a worthwhile solution.

Checklist for Publisher Project

Number	Section	Documentation	Done
1	Title page	**Student name, title of project and type of software**	
2	Identify (5 marks)	**Section title**	
3		Background detail	
4		User identified	
5		Statement of the problem	
6		Manual solution considered	
7		Two alternative software solutions considered	
8		Proposed solution justified	
9		At least 3 quantitative objectives identified	
10	Analyse (9 marks)	**Section title**	
11		Appropriate hardware identified	
12		Appropriate software identified	
13		Types and source of data explained (e.g. information from user, Internet research, clip art, scanned photographs)	
14		Data manipulation explained (e.g. image manipulation in a Paint package or spreadsheet/chart imported)	
15		Alternative methods of output considered (e.g. screen, printer)	
16		Choice of output method justified	
17		Backup strategy identified	
18		Security strategy explained	
19	Design (9 marks)	**Section title**	
20		Initial designs showing layout of pages, columns, graphics	
21		User feedback on initial designs (comments, letter or questionnaire results)	
22		Subtasks identified	
23		Each page sketched out showing content and placement of graphics, Fonts etc specified	
24		Test plan containing tests and expected results linked to user requirements in **Identify** section	
25	Implement (12 marks)	**Section Title**	
26		Brief description of how the design was implemented, explaining any changes that had to be made to the design	
27		Hard copy of publication(s), annotated to explain special features e.g. linked text boxes, text wrapped round graphics, images manipulated	
28		Evidence that each test in the test plan was carried out, comparing actual results with expected results	
29		When errors occurred, explain how they were corrected	
30	Evaluate (5 marks)	**Section Title**	
31		Each original objective fully evaluated. Comment on how well the objectives are fulfilled	
32		Comment on any major problems that caused a change in the design	
33		A critical comment on anything that you think could be improved	
34		User feedback in the form of a letter or questionnaire. User comment should be critical and relevant	
35		Evidence that you understand the user's comments by making suggestions for future improvements	

GCSE ICT Project

Desk Top Publishing

Sports Day Programme

Winner's Certificate

Template

Part One - Identify

Statement of the problem

As head of the PE department at Admiral High School, Mrs Whitehead is responsible for organising a sports day each year. The event involves pupils from all years and covers most of the events you would associate with an outdoor athletics competition. Usually, each event with its time is written up on blackboards around the field where the sports will be taking place. Here, athletes and spectators can see when they are next up for an event or when their sons, daughters or friends will be competing. This year, Mrs Whitehead wants me to design a professional-looking programme listing the events and event times for everyone to look at and keep after the occasion.

This project will also include a template for a winner's certificate. You should explain the need for certificates to give to the event winners. As before, mention why they are needed and what the school currently does for the winners.

Consideration of Alternative Solutions

- A programme and certificates could be designed and written up by hand and then photocopied the appropriate number of times. This would fulfill all of the content requirements of the PE department but may lack in quality of presentation.

- A word processor could be used to type up the programme and the certificates, including graphics and fancy headings. This would almost certainly be more professional-looking than the freehand method but a word-processing package does not provide the flexibility of a true desk top publishing package.

- *The most important alternative solution is the ICT solution using your chosen package – in this case it is MS Publisher. You need to state what features DTP software has that a word processor does not. You also need to state which of these features are applicable to solving your given problem.*

After consideration of each method I believe that MS Publisher offers the best solution to the problem because...

For top marks you need to summarise why the DTP solution is better than the others you have mentioned.

> Text in italics shows where you would need to insert extra documentation if this were your own project.

> Make sure that you show comparisons between each of the suggested solutions when you write your final justification for using Publisher.

User Requirements

The objectives of the design are as follows:

1. The programme must be convenient for visitors to carry around and refer to.

2. The programme needs to be printed on A4 paper so that it can easily be reproduced on a photocopier.

3. It must identify the school, the event and the date.

4. It must have a complete and accurate list of all of the events and event times.

5. The programme must include pictures from the previous year's sports event.

6. It must not contain any spelling or grammatical errors.

7. *You would need to add here some requirements for the certificates. Ideally, requirements should be measurably achievable (such as requirements 1 to 4) rather than "The certificate must look nice".*

> Try to think of between 8 and 10 good user requirements. This will give you more to talk about in the other sections of the project when you are required to refer back to these objectives.

Part Two - Analyse

Part Two - Analyse

Appropriate Software and Hardware

The software required to complete this programme will be Microsoft Publisher. I will also need a graphics package such as Paint Shop Pro to scan an image into. I can then import the image to Publisher. If I need to touch up any of the graphics to be included, this can also be done in Paint Shop Pro.

The hardware required will be the computer running the software, complete with monitor, keyboard and mouse for data entry and image manipulation. A scanner will be necessary to scan in any photographs that the department wants included in the leaflet.

A colour printer would also be required if the PE department want to see a colour copy of the programme. Since they will be reproducing it in black and white, I doubt that this will be necessary. A good quality greyscale printer such as a laser or inkjet will be fine.

If you need any other pieces of hardware or software, you must state what their purpose will be.

Data Required

Information about each of the events and the event times will need to be collected from the department. Images of last year's event can be scanned in from department photos. Where necessary the pictures will be opened in Paint Shop Pro where they can be cropped, touched up or saved as greyscale images for importing into the programme.

For added interest, information on world records can also be retrieved from the 'Guinness Book of World Records' website. Details of the school event records would also be interesting and are available from Mrs Whitehead. They can be displayed in a table for comparison.

Any previous attempts at programme design or the layout of the information on the blackboards at last year's events will also be useful in developing a good design. This information will also be available from the department.

You might also find some examples from outside sources of a Sports Day leaflet from which to borrow ideas.

> Importing a graphic into another package and manipulating it before you bring it into Publisher is a good way to help get your project into the 'Extension' level of the mark scheme.

> Think about every piece of information you are going to include and say where it will come from.

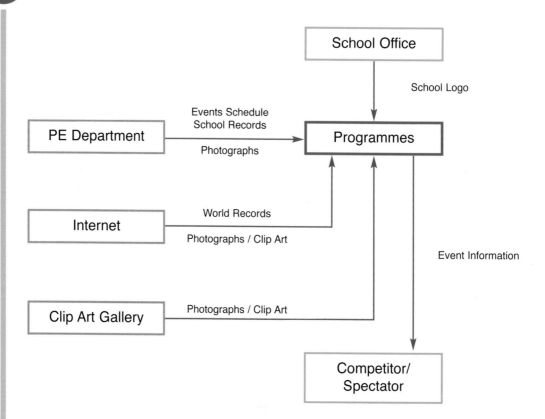

Format of information and graphics

In the programme, the text required will be a list of the events and start times. A list of school records and world record times will add more interest to each event. These will be displayed in a table in the programme and will be illustrated with graphics of the different sports events.

The graphics required will be pictures of sportsmen and women from the Internet or Clip Art galleries and a scanned photo belonging to the PE department. These will be sized appropriately so they fit into the space available. Graphics should not be distorted as this detracts from their original quality and may spoil the overall look of the final design.

The front cover should include the school's name and logo, and a title showing that this is the programme for the school Sports Day.

A blank area will need to be reserved for a sponsor's logo and company advertisement to be pasted in at a later date.

Describe here, in adequate detail, the format and layout of the certificates. You will need to consider what text and graphics will be required and how they might be arranged on the page.

Output

The programme will be created in Publisher and output in printed form for giving to spectators and athletes at Sports Day.

The final programme will be printed on thin card or ordinary paper. Thin card would be more durable but more difficult to fold. It would also be more expensive.

A colour design would be desirable but more expensive, and therefore the programmes will be printed on ordinary paper in greyscale rather than colour. This means that the reproduction of the programme can be done on site without the use of any special equipment. It can also be easily folded and will not be too bulky to carry around. Should card be desired at a later date, the original paper copy will be photocopied onto card.

State what form the certificates are likely to take once finished. It is likely that anything produced in a DTP package will need to be printed so you will need to include more detail. For example, what will it be printed on, how many copies per page, will it be in colour?

Backup / Security Strategy

The computer file containing the final designs must be backed up onto floppy disk at regular intervals. This copy should ideally be kept at a different location from the computer in case there is a fire or flood at the premises. Ideally a backup copy needs to be made each time more work is done on the programme.

Mrs Whitehead does not feel that there is any threat that the design will be tampered with so there is no need to password-protect it. It can be stored in a staff file area so that pupils cannot access it – the school's current levels of access already set up on the network will take care of this.

> Explain and fully justify your chosen method of backup and security. Even if security is not necessary, you will need to justify why.

Part Three - Design

Initial Designs

The programme will be either:

- a 2-fold design so that it is divided into 3 sections giving 6 pages, or

- 3 panels on 2 sides or a single fold design so that an A5 programme is created from an A4 sheet.

Ideas for initial design of programme

Having looked at the two different designs, I have decided that the single fold design is more practical since it provides a larger area in which to put text and pictures on each page. There is no need for 6 pages and both designs are small enough to fit into a pocket.

The initial designs of the programme are shown below and incorporate some of the ideas developed in the analysis of the task and also some ideas gathered in the research of other Sports Day programmes.

It was also decided that the design was best suited to a single-fold A5 format.

Your initial designs do not need to contain any great detail but should give the user a reasonable idea of what the final design might look like.

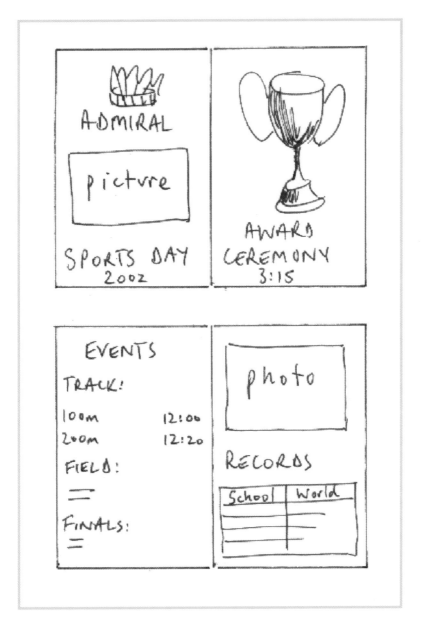

Initial design of programme (Pages 1-4-2-3) Version 2

Include at least one other design for the program. Only one is given here as an example of what is required. Further sketches for the certificates will also need to be included to give the user a good idea of how the certificate will look and enable her to make a reasoned judgement as to the suitability of each design. You do not need to include any great detail at this stage.

User Feedback on Initial Designs

The head of the PE department was given the programme designs to look at and made the following comments:

> "The first design has some good ideas and includes everything that it needs to but I like the order in which the information is set out in the second design."

> "The first design's front cover is most striking with the trophy but I would really like to use the trophy to complement the ceremony information. Perhaps this could be made smaller on the back cover. We could include a story about Richard Adams – I'll give you the information."

> "Will you be including more small graphics to brighten it up?"

> *You would also need to note down any comments made about your certificate designs here. Remember that you can use any method you like to collect feedback from the user.*

I will develop the second design further and make the desired changes as specified by the head of department.

Final Design

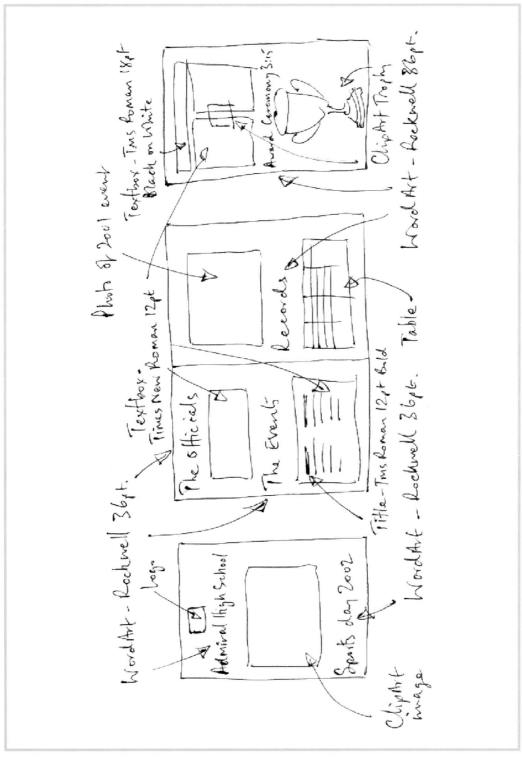

Textbox - Tms Roman 18pt Black on White

Award Ceremony 3:15

ClipArt Trophy

WordArt - Rockwell 36pt

Photo of 2001 event

Textbox - Times New Roman 12pt

Records

WordArt - Rockwell 36pt

Logo

Admiral High School

ClipArt image

The Officials

The Events

Title - Tms Roman 12pt Bold

WordArt - Rockwell 36pt

Table

Sports day 2002

In your own project design, show the leaflet full size and annotate it to show fonts, graphics and special features

Final design for programme

Schedule of Activities

The deadline for this project is in six weeks' time. A schedule of activities has been drawn up so that I keep to a strict timetable.

Week	Activity
Week One	Collect data and images from PE department and Internet. Sort out the useful bits and start to plan initial designs. Collect copy of school logo from school office.
Week Two	Continue planning initial designs and rough out on paper.
Week Three	Show initial designs to PE department for preliminary feedback. Update initial designs and decide upon one for development.
Week Four	Create final designs for programme and certificates.
Week Five	Implement final designs in MS Publisher. Devise test plan.
Week Six	Implement testing and evaluation. Finish off.

Test Plan

In order to make sure that the programme contains all the information required, that there are no errors and that it fulfils the requirements specified by the user, a test plan has been devised. This will be implemented once the designs have been finished.

Test	Description	Method of testing
1	Is the programme easy to carry around?	Fit the programme into a pocket.
2	Easily photocopiable?	Check that the programme is A4 size.
3	Full list of events and times?	Check the event list with the PE department.
4	Event photographs included?	Check with the department that the photograph included is from a previous year.
5	Spelling, grammar.	Run a spellchecker and proofread the entire programme.
6	Prints correctly	Print the programme and certificate and check that layout is correct.

This table shows how the project is broken down into more manageable sub-tasks.

Make sure that each test in the test plan adequately covers the original user requirements in the Identify section. This is how you can prove that you have met those objectives in the Evaluate section later on.

Your tests for Publisher will generally focus on more descriptive points such as spell-checking, proofreading and aesthetics.

You will also need to design tests for the Winner's Certificate template.

Part Four - Implement

Finished programme

Here is the finished programme shown in the sequence, page 1, 4, 2 & 3.

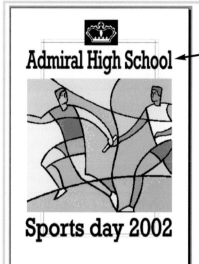

School logo, taken from website. School font used for 'Admiral High School' lettering

Heading spread across two columns

Text wrapped around graphic

Text boxes linked

Photo of last year's event, scanned and then cropped in Paint Shop Pro ready for importing into publication

Table inserted

Corrections in Design

More clip art pictures have been inserted to make the programme look more interesting. The story about Richard Adams has been laid out in 2 columns to make it look more like a news article. A clip art picture has been inserted between the columns with the text wrapped around it, which adds variety to the layout.

You need to include actual printouts of your publications. Obviously this cannot be done in this book. You should annotate your printouts to show how you implemented your designs and how clever you have been!

Make sure that any differences in your printouts from your final design are documented. It is perfectly normal to make last minute changes but you must say what they were and why they were made.

153

The list of events and times was rearranged to fit in three groups. This seemed easier to read and a better method to use when implementing the design. It also took up less space so a clip art picture could be added.

Test Results

Now that the final designs have been created, the test plan devised in the design section can be implemented. Reference to this plan should be made when reading the results below.

Your table of test results should follow on from the test plan plan that you made.

Test	Expected Result	Actual Result
1	Programme fits easily into an ordinary sized pocket.	Programme needed to be folded once to fit into most pockets but this was not thought to be a problem.
2	Programme is A4 size.	Programme measured up to exactly A4 size. (210mm x 297mm)
3	All events listed with correct times.	All information correct except that the Tug of War should start at 15:20 instead of 15:00. See figure below.
4	Suitable photograph selected and included in the programme.	Mr Smith said the photograph was an excellent choice.
5	Design contains no spelling and grammar mistakes.	Spelling errors in the word 'Meter' (American spelling) and Mr Warmington's name. Grammar fine. See figure below.
6	Prints correctly	A printout of the programme and certificate is shown earlier in this section.

It is important to include evidence of any errors that were corrected.

Error correction – Test 3

Scan in portion of programme where test 3 is fixed.

Part Five - Evaluate

Part Five - Evaluate

Evaluation of Initial Objectives

1. The programme is of a reasonable size so that all of the information it needs to contain is given plenty of space. It is small enough to fit into a pocket without being folded more than once. It is easy to find the information that you are looking for, since there is not too much of it and it is logically split up. Large headings describe each section.

2. A4 page layout has been used for the design so that it can be easily reproduced without the aid of a computer printer. This is because it is much cheaper for the school to copy a printout of the programme 500 times rather than print it 500 times. The programme can be photocopied 'back-to-back'.

3. All the events and event times have been listed by order of track and field events; unfortunately I feel that the event information could have been given slightly more space on the page and been organised in a better way. This is the only area of the programme design that is a little cramped, and since it is the most important information it should have been given more space.

4. There was only space for one picture of last year's races but it serves its purpose to generate excitement and anticipation of the event.

5. *Evaluate your other objectives in a similarly critical fashion.*

User Feedback on Solution

In order to get an accurate picture of the opinions of the actual users – in this case, the pupils of the school who will be using the programme, a questionnaire was given to a selection of them. An example of one of the questionnaires is shown on the next page.

> Make sure that you directly refer to the original user requirements in your evaluation.

> If you use a questionnaire for your feedback, it is a good idea to include some of the completed questionnaires.

Sports Day Programme 2001 – Questionnaire

Q1: Do you think that the layout is suitable for the
Sports Day programme?

Yes

Q2: Do you think that the programme will be easy for
you to carry around and refer to?

Yes

Q3: Is there any other information you would have
liked to see on the programme? If so, what?

Women's world records

Q4: Do you think that this is better than previous
solutions at getting the event information to
everyone involved?

Yes

Q5: What improvements would you suggest for the
programme?

Could be in colour.
Could have space to enter winners'
names.

Thank you for completing this questionnaire.

The answers on the rest of the questionnaires were gathered and the following feedback received:

1. All of those questioned thought that the design was appealing.

2. Everyone also thought that it would be very easy for them to carry around and added that they wouldn't think twice about having to carry it around.

3. The programme was generally easy to read, however one child said that the text was a bit too small for him to read since he has impaired vision. Other comments mentioned that the events list could be better designed.

4. The solution definitely proved to be better than the blackboards used in previous years.

5. Many suggestions for improvements said:

    "It would be nice to have it printed in colour."

Make sure that you get feedback on each of your publications if you have made more than one. In this case, feedback on the certificate would also be required.

Further Ideas for Improvements

In future years, the programme should be modified to include a space to write the winner's names in. This was a suggestion on one of the questionnaires and is quite a good idea. The programme could then be kept as a souvenir.

There were many suggestions for it to be in colour but this is too expensive for the school to produce. The programme could however be photocopied onto coloured paper. This would brighten it up without significantly increasing the cost.

Any further ideas for improvements should be based on the user feedback and your own opinions of the final publication.

Tips for implementation

This chapter will show you how to make the programme and certificate in Publisher. You can practise your skills using these instructions and refer back to them when you start your own project implementation.

Starting a new document

You may choose to use an existing template for your programme, or you could start with a blank page.

 Load Microsoft Publisher and select **Blank Page.**

Next you will need to set up the page size so that the programme can fit onto an A4 sheet, folded in half. Firstly, you may need to change the measurement units from inches to centimetres.

 From the **Tools** menu, select **Options**.

 Click the **General** tab and select **Centimeters** from the drop-down option box.

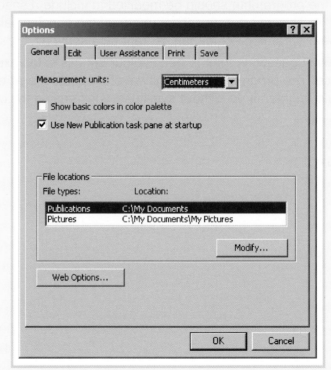

Figure 4.1: Changing the measurement units

 Click **OK**.

Page Layout

Now you can set up the page. An A4 sheet is about 21cm by 30cm. This is useful to know when checking that you have the right paper size selected.

 Click **File**, **Page Setup** on the main menu.

 Firstly, click on the **Printer & Paper** tab and check that you have **A4 (210 x 297mm)** paper selected from the Size box.

 Now click the **Layout** tab and select **Booklet** from the list of publication types.

 Make sure that the **Orientation** is set to **Landscape** and click **OK**.

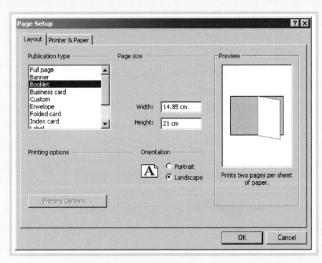

Figure 4.2: Adjusting the paper size

Publisher will ask you if you want to automatically insert another 3 pages. This will give you 4 pages in total on which to design your programme.

 Click **Yes** to insert pages.

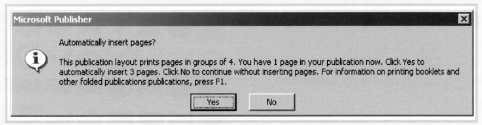

Figure 4.3: Automatically inserting pages

You should now see the first page displayed. Don't worry about the blue and pink lines on the page. These are margin lines and will not appear when the programme is printed.

Designing the front cover

The front cover has the school logo, some WordArt with the school name and some Clip Art of a sports event followed by some more WordArt saying "Sports Day 2002". The final designs in the Design section should already be complete and these will be used to implement the programme in Publisher.

The school logo for this programme could be copied from the school website or scanned in from some headed stationery.

 Find a suitable logo and insert it at the top of the front cover.

 Click the **WordArt** button and choose a suitable style. The second style has been chosen for this project. Adjustments can be made to the style later on.

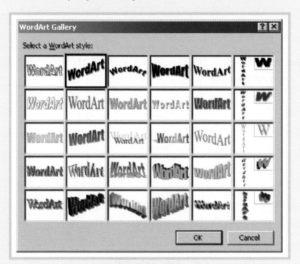

Figure 4.4

 Type *Admiral High School* in the **Edit WordArt Text** window.

 Select **Rockwell** as the font style and **36** for the size, then click **OK**.

 You can now use the WordArt toolbox to make any changes to the style. Click the **WordArt Shape** button on the toolbar.

 Select the first shape.

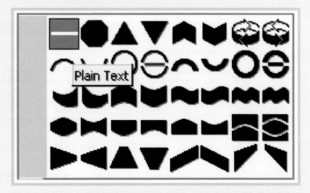

Figure 4.5: Selecting the shape of the WordArt

The top of your page should now look something like this.

Figure 4.6: The page so far...

Inserting Clip Art

Now you are ready to insert a picture into the centre of the page. The one for this cover comes from the Microsoft Clip Art Gallery Online.

▶ From the **Insert** menu, click **Picture**, **Clip Art...**

▶ Either find a suitable picture from the files on the computer you are using or click **Clips Online** on the taskbar to find an image on the Microsoft Clips Online website.

▶ When you have found a suitable sporting image, insert it into your programme.

▶ Insert some more WordArt underneath the picture saying *Sports Day 2002*.

Figure 4.7: The front cover

 Click **File**, **Save** to save the programme so far. Call it *Programme.pub*.

Adding the event information

The details of the event need to go on the inside pages of the programme. To do this you will need to view pages 2 and 3.

▶ Click the **Page 2** icon in the bottom left corner of the screen. Pages 2 and 3 will be displayed.

▶ Add some WordArt to say *The Officials* and place it in the top left corner of page 2.

▶ Now click the **Text Box** button on the Objects toolbar and drag out a rectangle below your new WordArt.

Figure 4.8: Adding a text box

▶ Fill in the text box with the list of officials running the event.

▶ Now create another piece of WordArt to say *The Events* and place this underneath the list of officials.

▶ Add 2 more text boxes and complete the list of events and event times as shown in Figure 4.9.

The Officials

Announcers:	Mr Warmington
	Mr Puls
Starter:	Mr Smith
Marks Person:	Mrs Whitehead
Timekeepers:	Mr Tyler
	Miss Bryan
Judges:	Mr Turner
	Mr Mongan
	Miss Salter

The Events

Track Events:

100 Metre Heats:	9:40
200 Metre Heats:	10:00
400 Metre Heats:	10:20
800 Metre Heats:	10:40
1500 Meter Heats:	11:00
4 x 100 Relay Heats:	11:20

Track Finals:

100 Metre Finals:	13:20
200 Metre Finals:	13:40
400 Metre Finals:	14:00
800 Metre Finals:	14:20
1500 Metre Finals:	14:40
4 x 100 Relay Finals:	15:00

Field Events/Finals:

High Jump:	11:40
Long Jump:	12:00
Javelin:	12:20
Discus:	12:40
Shot Put:	13:00
Tug of War:	15:00

Figure 4.9: Page 2

 Save your work.

Importing a graphic from a Paint package

This programme contains a photo of the races from last year's sports day. The photo was scanned into a Paint package and saved as a graphics file. It was then cropped in Paint Shop Pro before being imported into Publisher.

This is exactly the sort of thing that you should do for your own project to show that you manipulated a graphic in another application and then imported it. Make sure that you document properly any manipulation that you perform to get the full marks available.

Figure 4.10: Cropping an image

▶ From the menu bar, select **Insert**, **Picture**, **From File...**

▶ Browse through the directories on the computer you are using until you find the picture you need. Select the image and click **Insert**.

▶ Move the picture to the top of page 3 and drag out the corner to make it fill more of the width of the page.

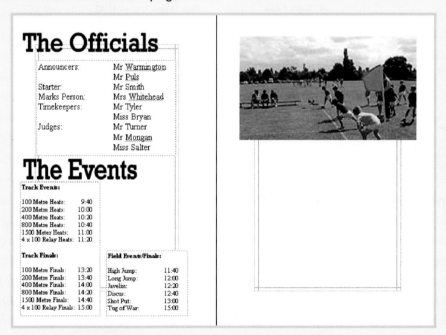

Figure 4.11: Inserting a picture from a file

Inserting a table

Underneath the picture you are going to add a table of past school records and world records for interest. Before you add this you will need to add another heading in WordArt.

▶ Use the WordArt tool to write the heading *Records* under the picture.

▶ Click **Table** on the main menu and then select **Insert**, **Table...**

▶ Increase the number of rows to **11** and choose **5** columns.

▶ Select the **Checkbook Register** style.

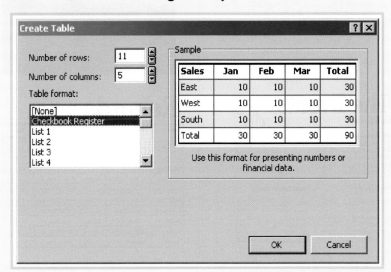

Figure 4.12: Inserting a table

▶ Click **OK**.

▶ Adjust the size of the table as necessary and complete it with the information given in Figure 4.13.

Records

Event	School Record Holder	School Record	World Record Holder	Men's Record
100 Metres	Richard Adams	10.7s	Maurice Green	9.79s
200 Metres	Richard Adams	21.7s	Frank Fredericks	19.92s
400 Metres	Christopher Deal	49.3s	Michael Johnson	43.18s
800 Metres	Geoffrey Marriott	2m 04s	Wilson Kipketer	1m 41.11s
1500 Metres	Sarah Jee	4m 52s	Hicham Guerrouj	3m 26s
High Jump	Michael Holton	1.55m	Javier Sotomayor	2.45m
Long Jump	Faria Karzai	6.10m	Mike Powell	8.95m
Javelin	Mark Reid	22.24m	Jan Zelezny	98.48m
Discus	William Ncube	17.87m	Jürgen Schult	74.08m
Shot Put	Matthew Deal	14.89m	Randy Barnes	23.12m

Figure 4.13: The records table

Inserting Clip Art illustrations

You can insert some smaller Clip Art graphics to help brighten up the pages if you wish. The ones shown below came from the Clip Art selection on Microsoft's Online Clip Gallery.

Figure 4.14: Pages 2 and 3

▶ Save the programme.

Creating the back page

The back page will contain a short article on the progress of an ex-pupil from the school and a notice about the awards ceremony at the end of the day.

▶ Click the **Page 4** icon to view the back page.

▶ Create a text box along the top of the page for the title of the article.

▶ Type *Admiral Athlete's Athens Adventure* as the heading.

▶ Change the font to **Times New Roman,** size 18.

▶ Select the text and click the **Fill Color** button. Fill the box in **Black.**

▶ With the text still selected, click the **Font Color** button and select **White.**

▶ Make 2 new text boxes underneath the heading as shown in Figure 4.15.

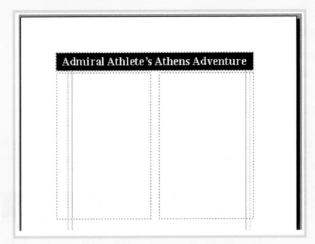

Figure 4.15

Linking text boxes

Linked text boxes will allow you to type text into one text box and automatically overflow any text that won't fit into another that it has been linked to.

First you must make sure that the Connect Frames toolbar is visible.

 Select **View**, **Toolbars** from the main menu and make sure that **Connect Frames** is checked. If it is not, click it.

Now you are ready to link the two text boxes.

 Click in the left hand text box.

 Now click the **Create Text Box Link** button on the Connect Frames toolbar.

 Move the mouse pointer over the right hand text box. It should turn into a jug of pouring letters. Click in the text box to create the link.

 In the first text box begin typing the following text. You should find that it will automatically spill over into the second text box because they have been linked.

> *Most of you will remember Richard Adams as one of last year's sixth form leavers and as outstanding star of many of our sports events. Since he left, he has been competing in several national and international athletics competitions and has just returned from the World Junior Championships in Barcelona where he won his first international medal, taking gold in the 200 metres.*
>
> *This year he has been devoting more time than ever to his fitness and we are proud to announce that he has recently been selected to join the British athletics team for training in preparation for the 2004 Olympic games in Athens. We wish him every success.*

Adding a graphic and wrapping text around it

Next you will need to find a graphic to add to the article. Sometimes the article text does not fit around the image properly so you will need to set this.

 Insert a picture of a runner from Clip Art.

Move it into the centre of the text, overlapping both text boxes, and size it similarly to the one shown below.

Figure 4.16

By default, the text should move out of the way for the image, but sometimes it will get covered up by it as in Figure 4.16. If this happens, you will need to adjust the wrapping.

 Select the image and click the **Text Wrapping** button on the **Picture** toolbar.

Figure 4.17

 Select **Square**. The text should now flow around the picture.

Adding borders

To finish off the programme, the award ceremony needs to be advertised. We will insert a Clip Art picture of a trophy within a BorderArt frame.

▶ Using the **Rectangle** tool on the **Drawing** toolbar, draw a rectangle to fill the bottom of the back page.

▶ Now double-click the rectangle to format it. The **Format Autoshape** window will appear.

▶ With the **Colors and Lines** tab visible, click the **BorderArt** button.

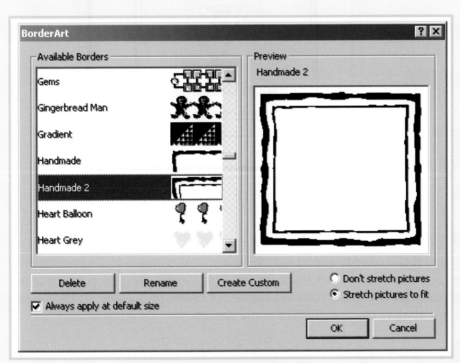

Figure 4.18: Adding BorderArt

▶ Select the **Handmade 2** design and click **OK**.

▶ Inside the border, add a Clip Art picture of a trophy and some WordArt to say *Award Ceremony Commences at 15:15*.

Figure 4.19: The back page

Setting graphics to grayscale

The user requirements stated that the programme needs to be photocopied many times on a black and white laser copier. This means that it is not necessary for the graphics to be in colour. They will come out better on a black and white copier if they are already black and white in the design.

 Select page 1.

 Click on the large image in the center of the page. The Picture toolbox should appear. (If it doesn't, right-click the image and select **Show Picture Toolbar** from the menu.)

The Color
button

Figure 4.20: The Picture toolbar

▶ Click the **Color** button on the Picture toolbar.

▶ Select **Grayscale**. The picture should turn to black and white.

▶ Repeat these steps with any other coloured graphics in your programme.

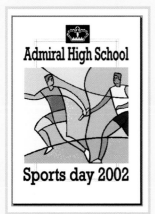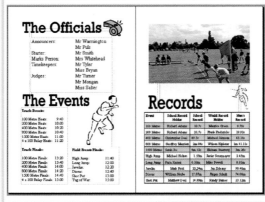

Figure 4.21: The finished programme

Implementing the Certificate template

The certificate is designed using exactly the same techniques that the programme uses, with the school logo, WordArt and borders. This certificate has a marble-effect background and is saved as a template rather than a normal file.

▶ With Publisher already open, click **File**, **New...** to create a new publication.

▶ Select **Blank Publication**. By default, the page size will already be set to A4, portrait style.

▶ Click **Format, Background...** The Background pane will appear.

*Figure 4.22:
Choosing a backgound*

 Select the **White Marble** design for the background.

 Now add the school logo and WordArt to the certificate as shown in Figure 4.23.

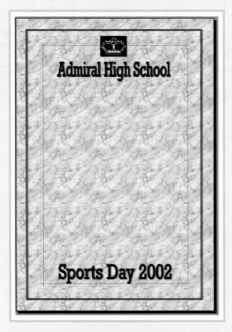

Figure 4.23

 Using the **Rectangle** tool, add a border around the certificate.

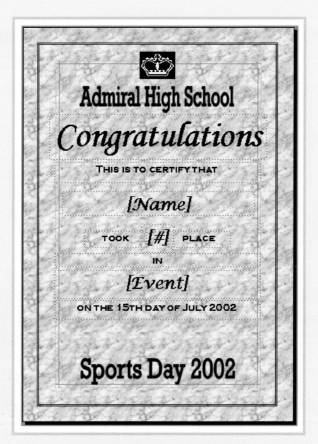

Figure 4.24: The certificate

 Add the rest of the text using the text box tool and format it appropriately. The *[Name], [#]* and *[Event]* textboxes will act as placeholders and are there to be replaced with the winner's name, placing and event. Make sure that these are formatted in the way you would like the names and events to be written on the certificate.

Saving a publication as a template

If you save the publication as a template, when you next open a new publication using the template to add the name, place and event for a student, the template itself will remain unchanged.

 Select **File**, **Save As...** from the main menu.

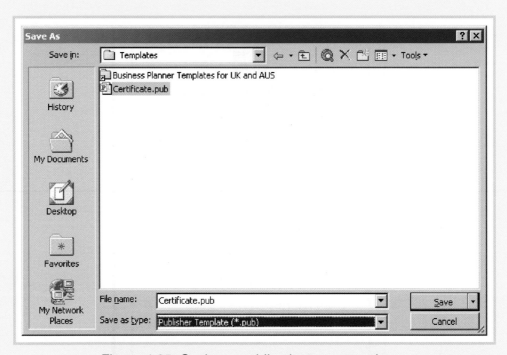

Figure 4.25: Saving a publication as a template

▶ Choose a suitable file name such as **Certificate** and in the **Save as type** box, select **Publisher Template (*.pub)**.

▶ Click **Save**. Your template should be saved in the Templates directory.

▶ Close the file.

Opening a file from a template

▶ Click **File**, **New...** from the main menu.

▶ In the New Publication task pane on the left hand side, click **From Template...**

▶ Publisher should automatically open the Templates directory where you saved your certificate template. Select **Certificate** and click **Create New**.

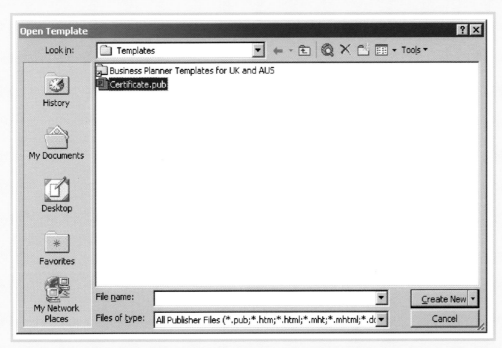

Figure 4.26: Opening a file from a template

 Your certificate will appear. Replace the *[Name], [#]* and *[Event]* placeholders with real names, places and events and print each one out.

Any changes you make to this file will not affect the template file you called **Certificate.pub.** This is the advantage of creating a template over a normal file.

Edexcel Coursework Assessment Criteria

Assessment Criteria

Levels of response for specific problem types

Problem type	Standard	Extension
Creation and Manipulation of a Database	Create the data files Search the database Sort the database Generate reports	Complex searches (eg and/or) Reports from more than one file Related tables Macros
Creation and Manipulation of a Spreadsheet	Enter text and numeric data Use of formulae Multiple sheets Printing Generate graphs	Multiple sheets with automatic transfer of data Complex formulae (eg if…) Look up tables Macros
Word Processing	Enter and edit text Font type and size Inserting clip art Page set up Columns Printing	Importation of data from another application Mail merge Setting up templates Macros
Desk Top Publishing	Enter and edit text Font type and size Inserting clip art Page set up Columns Printing	Importation of data from another application Text flow between blocks Image manipulation
Website Publishing	Enter and edit text Insert clip art Hyperlinks Font type and size Background	Importation of data from another application Image manipulation Web bots Forms CGI scripts Use of tables for layout

When marking, teachers should use the examples above as a guide to justify their marking for problem types not listed.

Assessment Criteria

Assessment criteria for the coursework collection

Standard and Extension	Assessment criteria	Evidence	Notes
0-1	A statement of the problem which is unclear or lacks detail.	*In order to do this, a student should provide:* Written evidence that outlines the problem that needs to be solved.	The 'real' user may need to be fictitious, but it should not be the student themselves. Role-play can be useful here with other students playing the role of 'real' users.
2-3	A clear statement of the problem which identifies the user(s). Consideration of possible alternative solutions. Objectives or user requirements should be stated.	Written evidence that clearly identifies the problem that needs to be solved and the user(s). Alternative solutions need to be considered. Objectives are stated in general terms.	Possible solutions could include a comparison of 'manual' methods with an ICT solution, stating why the ICT solution is preferred. In some cases it may be possible to suggest other software packages that could have been used to solve the problem.
4-5	A clear statement of the problem, giving some background detail and identifying the 'real' user(s). Consideration of possible alternative solutions with adequate justification given for the chosen method. Quantitative objectives or user requirements.	Written evidence that provides comprehensive details of the problem that needs to be solved and the 'real' user(s). Alternative solutions should be considered with justification for the proposed solution. Objectives will be quantitative. At least three quantitative objectives should be identified for the top marks.	Quantitative objectives, that can be measured, are much better for testing than objectives which are very general. *For example:* 'The user needs to be able to print out a list of stock that is out of date'. 'The user needs to send a letter to customer who has not paid his bill this week'. *Are preferable to:* 'The solution must be easy to use'.

Assessment Criteria

Analyse (9 marks)

0-2	0-3	Software identified. Raw data required has been partially identified. The output required has been identified. There is some explanation of how the data will be manipulated to solve the problem.	*In order to do this, a student should provide:* Software and hardware – explanation of what software is going to be used and why it is suitable for this problem.	A complete list of hardware is not necessary, only the hardware especially relevant to the problem, eg a scanner and colour printer for producing a magazine.
3-4	4-6	Software and hardware identified. The raw data required has been identified and its source and method of collection partially explained. Some explanation of the processing required. Flow of data through the system has been partially identified. Alternative forms of output have been considered and appropriate choices made. Backup and security strategies have been considered.	Analysis of the input data required, including source and methods of collection and error checking. Processing – how the data will be manipulated to solve the problem. Explanation of the flow of data through the system. Analysis of output requirements and formats.	Inclusion of details of any preparation of the data required before input and verification and/or validation procedures used. Diagrams may be a useful means of explanation. The flow of data through the system must be clear and explicit for full marks to be awarded. What output is going to be screen based and what data needs to be printed? Will different output be required at different times or in different situations? Will the output be sorted or a sub set of the data? What layout is needed?
5-6	7-9	Appropriate software and hardware identified. Data collection and input has been fully explained. Ways in which the data will be manipulated to solve the problem have been fully explained. The flow of data through the system is clear and explicit. Alternative forms of output have been considered and appropriate choices made and justified. Appropriate backup and security strategies have been identified and fully explained.	Analysis of strategies for backups and security.	A backup strategy suitable for the user should be clearly explained. Frequency, media, amount of data and time required to perform backup should be considered.

Assessment Criteria

Further guidance on 'Analyse'

Data required and its source

Examples

Database	Part numbers, descriptions and prices from a catalogue
Spreadsheet	Dates, customer names and total bill from invoices
Desk Top Publishing	Information about planets from encyclopaedia, picture of each from NASA website
Website Publishing	Details of car models from brochure and images obtained at club meeting with digital camera.

Data collection

This could be achieved using a form or questionnaire or by copying from the original source.

Data input

Selection of an appropriate method, eg keyboard, scanning and any verification or validation that is needed.

Data manipulation

Examples

Database	Fields required, outline of updates, searches, sorts, reports that will be needed
Spreadsheet	Calculations that need to be performed
Desk Top Publishing	Number of pages, columns, text required, graphics required
Website Publishing	Number of pages, links, text required, graphics required.

Flow of data

What is the sequence of operations needed to solve the problem? Flowcharts or other diagrams should normally be included. Reference should be made to the objectives/user requirements previously identified.

Output

What output is going to be screen based and what data needs to be printed? Alternative forms of output should be considered. Will different output be required at different times or in different situations? Will the output be sorted or a sub-set of the data?

Backup/security strategy

Examples

A weekly backup to floppy disk if the user has a simple set of accounts that they only update once a week; a daily backup to tape for a large database that has changes made to it every day.

The importance of security procedures will depend on the nature of the data being stored and the user. When password use is recommended, the user needs to be given guidelines about the effective use of this method of security.

Design (9 marks)

Standard	Extension	Assessment criteria	Evidence	Notes
0-2	0-3	Initial designs do not have enough detail for the user to make a judgement as to their suitability. No user's comments have been recorded. The final design contains little detail and the student would be unable to repeat the solution at a later date. No test plan.	*In order to do this, a student should provide:* Initial designs. User feedback on the initial designs. Final designs Test plans	Initial designs concentrating on look and feel. Comments from the user could be written on the initial design, or be in the form of a letter. If there were several users, a questionnaire could be used.
3-4	4-6	Initial designs are adequate for the user to get an idea of how the problem is to be solved. The user's comments have been recorded. The final design has enough detail for the student to carry out the solution, but not a competent third party. A test plan is present but does not fully test the problem.		Final designs should now take into account the user comments and contain all the detail needed to complete the task. The test plan devised should be linked to the objectives described in the 'Identify' section and any validation techniques used.
5-6	7-9	Initial designs are accurate enough for the user to make a reasoned judgement as to their suitability. The user's comments have been accurately recorded and acted on in the final design. The final design is described in such detail that a competent third party could implement the design. The proposed solution is broken down into manageable sub-tasks. A full and effective test plan has been devised, based on the previously identified objectives. Where validation techniques are planned, a full set of suitable test data has been devised.		

Further guidance on design

Data required and its source

Initial designs would typically be handwritten sketches without a lot of detail. They would be used to check with the user that the design roughly met their requirements. At this stage they would not be expected to include details such as formulae, search instructions or font sizes.

Taking the user's comments into account the student can then go on to put further detail into the design.

For example:

Database	File structures, validation details, clearly defined updates, sorts, searches, layout of screen forms and reports
Spreadsheet	Layout, formulae, validation details, macros
Desk Top Publishing	Page layout – positions of frames/columns/lines, fonts, text size, paragraph styles, position/size of graphics and blocks of text, links between frames
Website Publishing	Page layout, position of graphics/lines/tables, navigation buttons, clearly defined map of links.

Test plans

Database and Spreadsheet

Details of test data and a quantitative test plan are required. Tests with typical, extreme and invalid data.

For example:

Database	Test plan for searches, sorts and reports
Spreadsheet	Test plan for formulae.

Word Processing and Desk Top Publishing

The method of testing will be more descriptive, detailing the use of spellchecker, print preview, proof reading and aesthetic testing.

Website Publishing

Many of the tests for Word Processing and Desk Top Publishing are also suitable for this problem type. In addition, a test plan for links would be required.

Assessment Criteria

Implement (12 marks)

Standard	Extension	Assessment criteria	Evidence	Notes
0-2	0-3	A project that provides evidence that the software has been used, but bears little or no resemblance to the design and there is little or no evidence of testing.	*In order to do this, a student should provide:* **Annotated** hardcopy evidence of both implementation and testing, showing full details of the implementation process.	Whenever appropriate, the hardcopy evidence should be presented as if it had been produced by the user(s) using the system that has been implemented. It is not necessary to enter large amounts of data to simulate use of the implemented system, eg stock control with thousands of records. Approximately 20 realistic records should be adequate to demonstrate the system's use. If the final version differs from the original design, students should include some notes as to why the changes were necessary. Students should annotate their hardcopies to show the sequence of development, errors and areas for improvement. Testing should be annotated to show how the expected and actual results compare.
3-4	4-6	A project that provides evidence that the design has been implemented with some omissions. There is evidence that errors have been corrected and some unstructured testing has taken place.		
5-6	7-9	A project that provides evidence that the design has been implemented. Error correction has taken place and a test plan has been partially implemented or the test plan is not relevant to the problem.		
7-8	10-12	A project with evidence that the design has been fully implemented showing clearly that the problem has been solved. Evidence that all errors have been corrected and that a relevant test plan has been fully implemented.		

Assessment Criteria

Evaluate (5 marks)

Standard and Extension	Assessment criteria	Evidence	Notes
0-1	Evaluation is non-existent or weak with only general comments.	*In order to do this, a student should provide:* Written evidence of an evaluation of each of the objectives in the 'Identify' section. Evidence that the user has seen the problem's solution. Written evidence of further improvements.	Each of the original objectives should be evaluated as to whether they have been solved. Any problems the student had such as major changes to their design also need to be mentioned. Comments should be based on solving the problem not on the student's ability to use the software, etc. User feedback could be in the form of a letter or a questionnaire if there are multiple users. Critical and honest answers are much more useful to the student. The user feedback should lead the student into identifying further enhancements to the solution.
2-3	Evidence of evaluation against the objectives. User comments may be present but are too general.		
4-5	Original objectives are fully evaluated and the user comment is critical and relevant. There is evidence that the student has understood the user's comments and has suggested changes for the future.		

Index

	A	B	C	D	E
1					
2					
3					
4					
5					
6					
7					
8					
9					
10					
11					
12					
13					
14					
15					
16					